Living Through History

ELIZABETHAN ENGLAND

GEOFFREY REGAN

B.T. Batsford Ltd London

Contents

Typeset by Tek-Art Ltd, West Wickham, Kent
Printed and bound in Great Britain by
The Bath Press, Bath, Somerset
for the publishers
B.T. Batsford Ltd
4 Fitzhardinge Street
London W1H 0AH

ISBN 0 7134 6094 6

Acknowledgments

The Author and Publishers would like to thank the following for their kind permission to reproduce illustrations: The Marquess of Bath for figure 16; the Bodleian Library for figure 7; the British Museum for figures 6 and 25; City of Aberdeen for figure 23; the Courtauld Institute of Art for figure 1; Mary Evans Picture Library for figures 3, 5, 12, 17, 32, 35 and 41; the Pat Hodgson Library for the frontispiece and figures 4, 8, 11, 13, 18, 19, 21, 26-30, 33, 34, 37 and 39-45; the National Gallery of Ireland for figure 50; the National Galleries of Scotland for figure 24; the National Portrait Gallery for figure 14; and Col. Wingfield Digby, Sherbourne Castle for figure 2. All other illustrations are from the collection of the Publisher.

Frontispiece
An Elizabethan ale-house.

Cover Illustrations
The colour photograph shows a detail of the painted frieze from the Great Chamber, Gilling Castle (Bridgeman Art Library). The other illustrations show a Puritan family (Pat Hodgson Library) and Queen Elizabeth with the symbolic figure of Fame (Batsford archieves).

ELIZABETHAN ENGLAND

Rarely has any period in English history been so dominated by the personality of the ruling monarch as the Elizabethan. And yet few would have predicted such a golden future for Elizabeth. England at the end of Mary's unpopular reign, with its legacy of religious schism, a debt-ridden state and a war which was to lead to the loss of England's last possessions on the continent, was a poor inheritance. It was a state essentially medieval in government and outlook, in which localism was more important than nationalism and in which the great advances of the Italian Renaissance had had little effect. Armigail Waad, one of Elizabeth's early Privy Councillors, described England in 1558:

The queen poor, the realm exhausted, the nobility poor and decayed. Want of good captains and soldiers. The people out of order. Justice not executed. All things dear. Excess in meat, drink and apparel. Divisions among ourselves. Wars with France and Scotland. The French king bestriding the realm, having one foot in Calais and the other in Scotland. Steadfast enmity but no steadfast friendship abroad.

On to this unpromising stage, with its ragged and worn scenery, and its tired and backward-looking cast, came a young woman whose maturity belied her years.

. . . If ever any person had the gift or the style to win the hearts of people, it was this Queen . . . coupling mildness with majesty as she did, and in stately stooping to the meanest sort. All her faculties were in motion and every motion seemed a well-guided action; her eye was set upon one, her ear listened to another, her judgement ran upon a third . . . .

So said her tutor, Roger Ascham, who also described her learning:

The constitution of her mind is exempt from female weakness, and she is endued with a masculine power of application. No apprehension can be quicker than hers, no memory more retentive. French and Italian she speaks like English; Latin, with fluency, propriety and judgement; she also spoke Greek with me . . . .

A childhood of suffering and danger had taught her to mistrust the motives of all men

1 Queen Elizabeth, painted in 1585 by Nicholas Hilliard. Many of the portraits of Elizabeth painted after 1580 reflect the development of the cult of the Queen as Gloriana as well as the patriotic fervour which was built up to resist the threat of Catholic Spain.

and to rely instead on her own strengths and abilities. In an age when a queen was all too often merely a decoration which the king displayed to adorn his court, she was determined to rule as well as reign. No man would ever have the power over her that her father had used to condemn her mother, Anne Boleyn, to death.

Yet Elizabeth was willing to listen to good advice and act upon it. She was conservative in politics and derived her views from her humanist education under Roger Ascham as well as the traditions of the English monarchy. Necessary changes would only be carried through by the rule of law. She considered that her power came from God alone and yet she was prepared to be guided – but not ruled – by the advice of Parliament and her Privy Council.

I shall require you all, my lords, to be assistant to me; that I with my ruling, and you with your service, may make a good account to Almighty God . . . I mean to direct all mine actions by good advice and council.

As a woman (albeit a queen) in a man's world, Elizabeth knew the importance of exploiting her femininity to boost the mystique of monarchy on which she depended to keep in check her many powerful and ambitious courtiers. Her clothes were splendid and chosen with an eye to effect, so much so that throughout her reign poets and writers compared her flatteringly with history's renowned beauties. Above all she was their 'Gloriana', goddess and muse. Even as she aged and lost her looks her ego thrived on the adoration of her courtiers. She wore a different dress almost every day and when she died her chests contained some two thousand garments, many unworn.

The problems Elizabeth faced in 1558, on her accession to the throne, never entirely disappeared throughout her reign. Her greatness lay in the way she held off dangers

2 Queen Elizabeth being carried by her courtiers to attend a wedding. Her public appearances were always attended with as much splendour and ceremony as possible to cultivate the mystique of the monarchy and distance her from her subjects.

which would have broken lesser rulers. As the last of Henry VIII's children she knew the importance of securing the succession and yet she resisted marriage which alone could have guaranteed that Henry's line continued. In foreign affairs she was able to use the prospect of her own marriage as a weapon of diplomacy, keeping the princes of Europe guessing and keeping as many of her options open as she possibly could. When pressed by Parliament to marry, she repied

Yea, to satisfy you, I have already joined myself in marriage to a husband – namely, the kingdom of England.

Allied to government problems abroad was the ever-present spectre of national bankruptcy. One of Elizabeth's greatest achievements was the revaluation of the coinage. Acting on this advice from Sir Thomas Gresham and William Cecil she restored her credit at a time when others like Philip II of Spain were courting bankruptcy:

FRANCISCVS VALESIVS D G DVX ALENSON ET
BRABANT COMES FLANDRIÆ PROTECT: BELGICÆ.

3 François, Duke d'Alençon, was probably the most serious of all Elizabeth's foreign suitors but the proposed marriage was unpopular in England, particularly with the Queen's Puritan subjects.

It may please your Majesty to understand, that the first occasion of the fall of the exchange did grow by the King's Majesty, your late father, in abasing his coins from six ounces fine to three ounces fine . . . whereupon . . . all your fine gold was conveyed out of this your realm . . . . To restore your realm . . . your Highness hath no other ways . . . but to bring your base money into fine of six ounces . . . to keep up your credit, and especially with your own merchants . . . .

In an inflationary period foreign wars were too expensive for any state and Elizabeth was prepared to use every means at her disposal to avoid the drain on her finances that foreign commitments would bring. Even when war with Spain became unavoidable in 1585, Elizabeth kept a tight control on her commander Leicester's expenditure.

Elizabeth was the living symbol of her father's break with Rome, since Henry had divorced his first wife, Catherine of Aragon, in order to marry Elizabeth's mother, Anne Boleyn. However she had no intention of being a slave to the extreme Protestants who flooded back to England from Germany on the news of her sister's death, which had signalled the end of religious persecution during Mary's Catholic reign. Catholics might claim fearfully that "the wolves will be coming out of Geneva . . . full of pestilent doctrines", but Elizabeth had no intention of letting them feed on her flock. She wanted a moderate church in which all men could find salvation, outwardly conforming even if inwardly they still held to the religion of their ancestors. Elizabeth insisted she

. . . never had any meaning or intent that her subjects should be troubled or molested by examination or inquisition in any matter of their faith . . . or for matters of ceremonies, as long as they shall in their outward conversation show themselves quiet and not manifestly repugnant to the laws of the realm.

Yet she could not avoid the religious turmoil of the Counter-Reformation completely. Determined to steer an even course between what she saw as the ungodly excesses of

4 The Puritans wanted to purify the Church of England of all Romanish superstitions and objected to the ceremonies and rituals of the new Church and the vestments worn by Anglican ministers. They lived simple lives, rejecting luxury and entertainments, and as a result were often ridiculed in Elizabethan and later in Jacobean literature.

5 Burghley House, built between 1552 and 1587, incorporates both Gothic and Renaissance architectural elements. The Elizabethan period saw a great deal of house building which reflected the confidence felt by her courtiers of the security of England under Elizabeth.

Calvin's Geneva and the threats posed by Roman Catholicism to her national church, Elizabeth was forced to take ever more vigorous measures to suppress religious dissent. In the process some innocent men were bound to suffer and the case of Edmund Campion was a particularly tragic example.

Elizabeth's reign saw not only the rise of Puritanism, notably in the merchant communities of the south and east of England, but also their increasing activity in Parliament. Elizabeth tried to control matters in the two houses of Parliament by ensuring that at least some of her Privy Councillors were members and were able to influence debates and represent "government" policy. On several occasions she clashed with her members of parliament, notably on religion, the succession and how she should treat Mary Queen of Scots. Elizabeth refused to be bullied and made it clear that parliamentary freedom did not extend as far as criticizing or commenting on royal decisions. Her popularity and the diplomatic skill of her councillors enabled her to frustrate parliamentary efforts to gain

supremacy throughout her reign. However, her successors were not to be so fortunate.

The internal security of England, particularly after 1570, enabled wealthy men to direct their attention away from war and the defence of the realm towards the pursuits of peace and patronage of the arts. The Elizabethan age was a "golden age" which saw an inspired output of literature, poetry and drama. There was also an unprecedented outburst of house-building. Prominent courtiers like Burghley, Leicester and Hatton built magnificent houses as symbols of their new confidence in England.

In maritime exploration England had to make up for a late start. During the previous century Spain and Portugal had divided the world between them, Spain claiming a monopoly in the Americas while Portugal claimed Africa and the East. At the beginning of Elizabeth's reign English mariners and traders looked for a way to reach the Indies and China by way of a north-east or north-west passage. Willoughby and Chancellor tried the route round the north cape of Norway to Russia, while Martin Frobisher and later John Davis attempted the north-west passage into the arctic regions of modern Canada. Inspired as much by the hope of vast riches as well as exploration, these voyages were financed by courtiers as well as the Queen herself. The explorers themselves benefited from the maps and geographical knowledge of men like John Dee and Richard Hakluyt. The latter believed English colonization of North America could pave the way for a British empire to rival that of Spain. Unhappily, Hawkins and Drake chose to break the Spanish slave monopoly. Later, Drake's circumnavigation established Britain's credentials as a major sea power. In the later part of Elizabeth's reign, Ralegh, Gilbert and Grenville laid foundations for the English colonization of the east coast of North America.

6 A contemporary map by Flemish mapmaker Josse de Hondt showing both the first English circumnavigation of the world by Drake and the second by Thomas Cavendish.

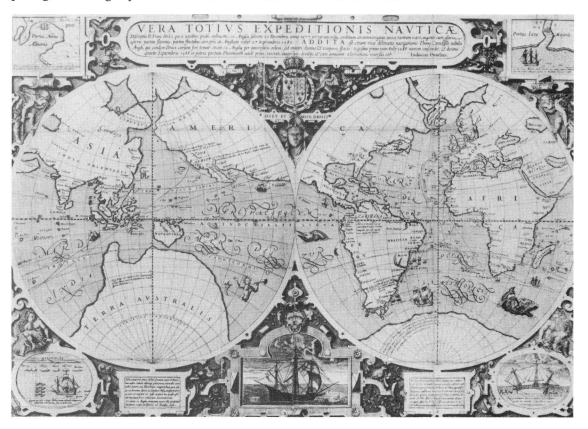

ELIZABETHAN GOVERNMENT, LAW AND ORDER

In 1558 England needed a strong central government. At the centre Elizabeth became the source of power and her selected ministers were also her courtiers. Wherever she was, whether at a royal palace or on a progress in the south of England, there also was the court and the centre of government. Patronage was power and Elizabeth was the greatest patron, giving appointments to those who pleased her or whose advice she valued. These she might appoint to her Privy Council, though not every favourite became a councillor as Ralegh found.

Elizabeth had a much smaller Privy Council than her sister Mary, perhaps between 12 and 20 members, whose task was to advise her. Although different shades of opinion were represented, it was not until late in her reign that real factions developed around men like Essex and Robert Cecil. Although there was no equivalent of the modern Prime Minister, certain councillors had the ability, or influence with the Queen, to dominate discussions, like William Cecil or Robert Dudley.

Parliament consisted of two houses, the Lords and the Commons, and some of Elizabeth's councillors were members of both houses. Its main function was to raise money to enable the Queen to carry out policy, as well as to pass laws. Political parties did not exist but during the reign pressure groups, notably the Puritans, pressed for policies which Elizabeth was not prepared to grant.

In local affairs, Elizabeth depended on the work of the Justices of the Peace, who met four times a year in quarterly sessions to deal with minor offences. In the absence of a national police force it was often difficult to bring a swift end to the career of criminals like Gamaliel Ratsey.

William Cecil, Lord Burghley (1520-98)

The fact that Elizabeth inherited an essentially medieval state and bequeathed her successor a more modern one, owed much to the work of the greatest statesman of the sixteenth century, William Cecil. The picture of an aging queen sitting at the bedside of the dying Cecil, feeding the old man with her own hand, tells us much about the real Elizabeth and her relationship with her minister. And when Cecil was suffering from gout, Elizabeth allowed him to sit in her presence:

My lord, we make use of you, not for your bad legs, but for your good head.

Elizabeth loved the quiet family-man in William Cecil, as well as the brilliant statesman. She knew all sides of her great minister as he knew her, both as queen and woman, sometimes coldly regal and sometimes wildly impulsive. He knew how to sail the ship of state in the way that made the most of Elizabeth's enormous energies. Yet Cecil

7 Lord Burghley in old age riding his mule. Elizabeth continued to rely on him rather than her younger favourites like Essex and Ralegh.

This judgement I have of you, that you will not be corrupted with any manner of gift, and that you will be faithful to the state, and that without respect to my private will, you will give me that counsel that you think best . . . .

During the next 40 years Cecil held a series of high positions, in all of which he achieved outstanding results. Until 1572 he remained Principal Secretary of State, afterwards until his death being Lord Treasurer. In addition, from 1561-1598 he was Master of the Court of Wards, the principal area of court patronage, and also Chancellor of Cambridge University. Cecil's influence was immense, second only to that of the monarch.

From the start Elizabeth gave Cecil her trust and he never betrayed it. He saw in her

. . . the wisest woman that ever was, for she understood the interests and dispositions of all the princes in her time, and was so perfect in the knowledge of her own realm, that no councillor she had could tell her anything she did not know before . . . .

also knew the hollowness of rank and power and looked beyond both his own life and that of his Queen, working ceaselessly to ensure a secure succession for his son Robert and for James VI of Scotland. One picture shows Cecil in old age, suffering from gout and humbly riding a mule because a horse pained him too much. Yet in a court dominated by arrogant and brilliant men, Cecil on his mule was master of them all.

Born in 1520 in Lincolnshire, William was an able scholar at Cambridge, friendly with such men as Cheke and Ascham. A firm but moderate Protestant, William's interests turned towards politics and the law, and his marriage to the wealthy Mildred Cooke brought him contacts that would further his career. He served under both Henry VIII and his son Edward, and managed the real estate for the young Princess Elizabeth. By the death of Mary, William already had a reputation as a shrewd politician and it was no surprise when the young Elizabeth chose him as her chief minister on her accession in 1558.

Their partnership worked best when they sank their differences but if Elizabeth could not agree with Cecil then hers would be the last word. He knew how uncertain her temper could be, described here by the Scottish Ambassador:

Her temper was so bad that no Councillor dared to mention business to her, and when even Cecil did so she had told him that she had been strong enough to lift him out of the dirt, and she was able to cast him down again.

In such situations, Cecil found it best to approach her indirectly, through lengthy memoranda or through a favourite like Leicester or Hatton. They agreed on what was best for the country in terms of strong government, a religion in which every man could find a place, and financial security. On only two occasions did Cecil find it necessary to force Elizabeth's hand: in 1561 he pressured her into driving the French out of Scotland and, in 1587, he moved heaven and earth to make her sign Mary Stuart's death warrant. In the second case, he earned her anger more severely than at any time. But it was a burden which he was prepared to bear. If every document leading to the execution of Mary Stuart carried the signatures of the Privy Council the prime mover was undoubtedly Cecil. He knew that he spoke for the majority of clear-thinking Englishmen in demanding the death of the Queen of Scots.

To express her many attempts both for the destruction of the Queen's person and the invasion of this realm, that the hope and comforts she has given to the principal traitors of this realm, both abroad and here at home . . . she is justly condemned to die. The whole realm has often times vehemently required that justice be done, which her Majesty cannot longer delay.

When news of Mary's execution reached Elizabeth, her rage was ungovernable. Although Secretary Davison was the main scapegoat, Burghley did not escape unscathed. He wrote to the Queen pleading for her forgiveness:

. . . for this late fact [the execution of Mary], for which your Majesty is deeply offended, I am no more to be charged than others, yet I find and hear by report that your Majesty doth with more bitter terms of displeasure condemn me than others.

How genuinely angry Elizabeth was with her ministers and how sorry for the death of Mary Stuart we will never know. In the end Burghley was reconciled with the Queen and restored to favour, but as he knew, it had been a close thing.

As Elizabeth's Principal Secretary, Cecil was the head of the administration of both domestic and foreign policy. In the latter he favoured friendship with Spain, though a Protestant himself, because he feared French ambitions on the coasts opposite England. In this respect he made enemies not only of men like Leicester who hated the idea of a Spanish alliance but also the older nobles like Norfolk who felt him an upstart. Through the agency

8 Sir Francis Walsingham was one of Elizabeth's most trusted advisers. His network of spies inside England and on the Continent kept him informed of Catholic plots to overthrow the Queen and replace her with Mary Stuart.

of Walsingham, with his spy network throughout Europe, Cecil kept himself well-informed of affairs in all the royal courts. This won him few friends abroad. Here is a very hostile view of Cecil by the Spanish ambassador, de Spes:

Lord Burghley . . . is a man of mean sort, but very astute, false, lying and full of all artifice. He is a great heretic and such a clownish Englishman as to believe that all the Christian princes together are not able to injure the sovereign of this country . . . .

After the collapse of the Ridolfi Plot (see page 18) in 1571 Cecil was made Lord Burghley and the following year Lord Treasurer. During the 1570s the Privy Council became increasingly divided over foreign affairs, with a Puritan group under Leicester and Walsingham pressing Elizabeth to become the head of a Protestant League against Spain and the Pope, while moderates under Burghley pressed for non-involvement in the Netherlands. During this time financial stringency meant that Elizabeth and Burghley were in agreement that war was too expensive. However, after the assassination of William of Orange (leader of the Dutch revolt against Spanish rule) in 1584, even Burghley knew that if England did not intervene then a Spanish victory in the Netherlands was certain. This would encourage Catholics everywhere and make it even more likely that an attempt would be made to overthrow Elizabeth and replace her by the Catholic Mary Stuart. Once forced off the fence, Burghley became the principal spokesman for his country, answering Spanish claims with the powerful invective he rarely used in council.

In religious affairs Cecil, though sharing some ideas with the Puritans, was a supporter of the Anglican Settlement of 1559, working throughout his life for the "middle way". As the Catholic threat developed during the 1580s Cecil favoured strong measures against Jesuit missionaries, employing "The Bloody Question" (see page 37) to trap many Catholic priests and condemn them to death. To Cecil the issue was not a spiritual one. He did not hate the individual priests, only what they represented – namely the power of the Catholic Church and Spain, which threatened the survival of England.

. . . there could be no government where there was division. And that state could never be in safety where there was toleration of two religions. For there is no enmity so great as that for religion. And they that differ in their service of God can never agree in the service of their country.

The last decade of his life saw his body weaken but his mind remain remarkably clear. He entertained Elizabeth lavishly at his two great houses, Burghley and Theobalds,

9 Lord Burghley and his son Robert Cecil, whom he groomed to succeed him as head of Elizabeth's Council.

and prepared his son Robert to succeed him when the time came. His advice to Robert in the 1580s was as sound as ever.

Towards thy superiors be humble yet generous; with thy equals familiar yet respective; towards inferiors show much humility and some familiarity . . . . Yet I do advise thee not to affect nor to neglect popularity too much. Seek not to be E. [Essex] and shun to be R. [Ralegh].

His death in 1598, though greatly mourned, provided no more than a ripple on the surface of affairs, which he had done so much to keep smooth. The peaceful accession of James I in 1603 was a triumph not only for Robert Cecil but for his father. At his death Ben Jonson wrote,

The only faithful Watchman for the realm, That in all tempests never quit the helm . . . .

Robert Dudley, Earl of Leicester (1532-88)

Historians have not been kind to Robert Dudley. This is what some of them have said about him:

"England indeed was well rid of him."
"Leicester represented all that was worst in the politics and culture of the English Renaissance."
"Robert Dudley stood for no one except Robert Dudley."
"A handsome, vigorous man with very little sense."

Yet for all his faults Robert Dudley was trusted by his Queen, a woman of great intelligence and perception. Perhaps there is something the historians are missing? When Elizabeth chose not to marry she needed a man to carry out many regal functions. In this sense throughout the reign Dudley was, in fact if not in name, the royal consort. He presided with her at court banquets and revels, tournaments and ceremonials, acting as a link between Elizabeth and her council. She trusted him and liked his company. None of her later favourites got as close to her heart as "Sweet Robin" or her "eyes", as she called him.

10 Robert Dudley, Earl of Leicester, though descended from a "tribe of traitors" (both his father and his brother had been executed) proved to be one of Elizabeth's closest advisers.

Robert had been Elizabeth's childhood playmate and had shared the tuition of Humanist Roger Ascham, but when his father Northumberland fell from power in 1554 he was sent with him to the Tower under sentence of death. Although his life was spared by Queen Mary his fortune was gone

and he took military service in France, distinguishing himself fighting the French. From an early age Robert had learned to live by his wits and realizing Catholic Mary was dying he looked for advancement to her sister Elizabeth.

Elizabeth had never lost her childhood attraction to handsome Robert Dudley and as Queen she rewarded him with high office, first as Master of the Horse, then Knight of the Garter, and finally, while she was suffering from smallpox in 1562, proclaiming him Protector of the Realm. Naunton describes Robert like this:

He was a very goodly person, tall and singularly well featured, and all his youth well favoured, of a sweet aspect . . . .

Elizabeth called Robert her "eyes" and paid him such attention that the rumour was that he was her lover and that she would marry him. In 1559 Count de Feria wrote,

During the last few days Lord Robert Dudley has come so much into favour that he does whatever he likes with affairs and it is even said that Her Majesty visits him in his chamber day and night. People talk of this so freely that they go so far as to say that his wife has a malady in one of her breasts and the Queen is only waiting for her to die to marry Lord Robert.

Robert's closeness to the Queen won him enemies, as a Spanish Ambassador noted.

The Duke of Norfolk is the chief of Lord Robert's enemies, who are all the principal people in the kingdom . . . he said that if Lord Robert did not abandon his present pretensions and presumptions he would not die in his bed . . . .

The mysterious death of Robert's wife, Amy Robsart, who fell down some stairs and broke her neck, caused a scandal which involved the Queen. Although a jury returned a verdict of accidental death, scandalmongers said Robert had killed her so he could marry the Queen. Mary Stuart in France was beside herself with laughter.

The Queen of England is going to marry her Horsekeeper who has killed his wife to make room for her.

Robert was deeply shocked, not so much because he had loved Amy but because of the way his enemies would use her death to harm him.

I have no way to purge myself of the malicious talk that I know the wicked world will use.

Yet Elizabeth did not lose faith in him.

. . . the matter has been tried in the country . . . and neither touches his honesty nor her honour.

To confirm her support she appointed him as a Privy Councillor and granted him the splendid Kenilworth Castle.

While Elizabeth used the question of her marriage as a political weapon, to keep foreign princes guessing, Robert pursued his amorous adventures with Lettice Knollys and Lady

11 Kenilworth Castle, granted by Elizabeth to Robert Dudley in 1563, in which Dudley provided the most splendid entertainments of the age.

Douglas Sheffield, which infuriated the jealous Queen. After marrying Lettice Knollys, a woman Elizabeth hated, in 1578, Robert endured the Queen's wrath for marrying the "she-wolf" and was almost sent to the Tower. The stormy relationship between the childhood playmates continued throughout their lives and it is clear that if Elizabeth loved anyone it was probably Robert Dudley.

Robert was one of the most splendid of Elizabeth's courtiers, dressing in dazzling clothes and aping the latest continental fashions.

Touching the silks I wrote you about, I wish you to take up and stay for me 4000 crowns worth of crimson and black velvet and satins and silks of other colours.

He dressed to impress regardless of cost.

I . . . have lived always above any living I had.

For the Queen's visit to Kenilworth in 1575, Robert prepared the most lavish social event of the age. It may be that young William Shakespeare witnessed the revels and these found a part later in *A Midsummer Night's Dream*. Robert was a patron of poets like Spenser and also set up a company of players, including James Burbage, known as "Lord Leicester's Men". In this way Robert was the prime mover and certainly the greatest patron of the English Renaissance, helping pre-Shakespearean writers like Marlowe, Greene, Nashe and Peele to make the theatre a respectable form of entertainment.

Robert came from the foremost Protestant family in England and was proud to be a patron of the Church.

Look for all the bishops that I have commended to that dignity . . . . Look of all the deans that have been commanded by me . . . who in England hath more learned chaplains belonging to him than I or hath preferred more learned preachers? Where have I ever refused any one preacher or good minister to do for him the best I could?

In the Privy Council, with Walsingham, he led the anti-Spanish group, pressing for an alliance of Protestant states led by England to combat Spanish power abroad.

. . . Leicester, Hatton and Walsingham have endeavoured to persuade the Queen that it is desirable for her to openly take the states [the Netherlands] under her protection . . . but they have been opposed by Cecil and Sussex when the matter was discussed in the Council . . . .

At home Robert constantly warned Elizabeth of the Catholic threat.

Nothing in the world grieves me more than to see her Majesty believes that this increase of Papists in her realm can be no danger to her . . . . If she suffers this increase but one year more . . . it will be too late to give or take cousel to help it.

With other leading councillors he organized the Bond of Association of 1584, pledging to pursue to the death anyone who tried to assassinate Elizabeth. As a result Robert was a target for Catholic loathing throughout Elizabeth's reign.

Robert had military ambitions which he hoped to satisfy by leading English forces to fight Spain in the Netherlands. In 1585 Elizabeth appointed him Commander of the English expeditionary force sent there after the assassination of William of Orange, and he received a great welcome from the Dutch which turned his head so that he accepted the title of Governor General, contrary to the Queen's orders. Elizabeth heard the news not from Robert but from one of her women who had heard that Lettice, Robert's wife, was going to Holland,

. . . with such a train of ladies and gentlewomen, and such rich coaches, litters and side-saddles as her majesty had none such . . . and she would set up such a court of ladies as should far pass her majesty's court.

Elizabeth was enraged and wrote to Robert

How contemptuously we conceive ourself to

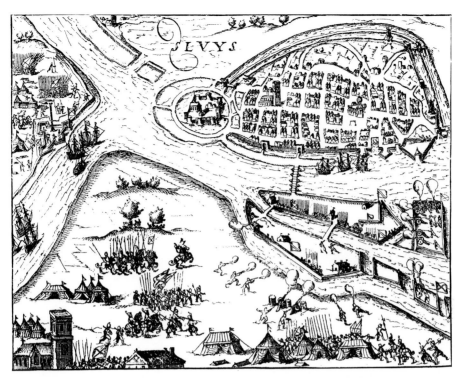

12 The besieged town of Sluis in the Netherlands. The expedition sent by Elizabeth to the Netherlands in 1585 demonstrated the Queen's commitment to the cause of Dutch independence from Spanish rule.

have been used by you, you shall by this bearer understand . . . . We could not have imagined . . . that a man raised up by ourself and extra-ordinarily favoured by us above any other subject of this land, would have in so contempt-ible sort have broken our commandment . . . .

Robert's handling of the campaign had been inefficient and he had vastly overspent his resources, but he knew how to win back Elizabeth's affection. When he sent back a messenger to report that he was sick, a device he had used before, Elizabeth's anger melted and he was soon her "Sweet Robin" again. In July 1586 she was once again writing affectionately to her "eyes".

Rob, I am afraid you will suppose by my wandering writings that a midsummer moon hath taken large possession of my brains this month . . . .

With the Armada certain to leave Spain in 1588, Elizabeth turned to her old friend, now failing in health and suffering from malaria. For the last time he answered the call and took command of English land forces awaiting the Spaniards at Tilbury. In this dire emergency Elizabeth considered, as she had in 1562 drawing up a patent naming Robert Lieutenant-Governor of England and Ireland. Only the strongest arguments from Burghley, fearful of the threat to her royal supremacy, prevented her doing so. In the event, it would have counted for little as Robert Dudley died shortly afterwards and was buried at Warwick. Elizabeth was genuinely saddened by the loss but a Spanish observer commented,

. . . no other person in the country shared the Queen's sense of loss.

Perhaps this was not quite true yet the poet Spenser, loyal to his old patron, wrote of those who had benefited from his help:

His name is worn already out of thought.
Nor any poet seeks him to revive,
Yet many poets honoured him alive.

Thomas Howard, Duke of Norfolk (1536-72)

13 Thomas Howard, Duke of Norfolk. His plan to marry Mary Stuart provoked the Northern Revolt in 1570 and he was later involved in the Ridolfi plot and ended his days on the block.

As Duke of Norfolk, Thomas Howard's power, particularly in East Anglia, was something Elizabeth had to harness, for by blood he was her cousin and connected to every noble family in the realm. From his palace in Norwich, Norfolk must have felt almost like a king, with county families owing him allegiance stronger than they felt for the monarch in London. Through patronage Thomas controlled justice and parliamentary elections in East Anglia and Elizabeth knew she must rule either through Thomas Howard or else she would have to break him.

When Mary Stuart fled to England in 1568, Norfolk was appointed to head the Commission at York which inquired into the dispute between the Scottish Queen and her subjects. He was shown the Casket Letters by Moray, Regent for the young James I of Scotland, and these love letters, written by

Mary to the Earl of Bothwell (see page 27), convinced him of Mary's guilt. He wrote to Elizabeth,

... the said letters and ballads ... do discover such inordinate love between her and Bothwell, her loathsomeness and abhorring of her husband that was murdered.

Yet Norfolk was an ambitious man and, while at York, it was secretly suggested to him that he might marry Mary Stuart, restoring her to the throne of Scotland and eventually succeeding to the throne of England. When rumours of this proposal reached Elizabeth's ears she confronted Norfolk who assured her of his "vehement misliking of such a marriage". Norfolk knew he was being tested and added,

... no reason could move him to like of her that hath been a competitor to the Crown; and if Her Majesty would move him thereunto he will rather be committed to the Tower, for he meant never to marry with such a person, where he could not be sure of his pillow.

In spite of such protestations, perhaps even because of them, the idea of marriage to Mary Stuart became even more attractive to him.

During 1569, Norfolk joined other Privy Councillors in plotting to overthrow William Cecil. The previous year Spanish bullion ships carrying Genoese gold to pay the Duke of Alva's troops in the Netherlands had been forced to seek refuge in English ports, whereupon the gold had been seized on Cecil's orders. The Spanish retaliated with an embargo on English goods which made Cecil very unpopular among city merchants. Cecil's chief opponent was Robert Dudley, who hoped to use this present unpopularity to end Cecil's 10-year rule, while Thomas Howard had his own reasons for wanting to see Cecil fall, Cecil being, he knew, the arch-enemy of

14 Mary Stuart, who was forced to flee to England in 1568 and became a focus for those discontented with Elizabeth's reign. Elizabeth called her cousin "the Daughter of Debate".

Mary Queen of Scots. Norfolk used a Florentine banker, Ridolfi, as a go-between to contact the Spanish ambassador, assuring the latter that the impounded gold would soon be returned. Meanwhile, the plotters moved to overthrow Secretary Cecil.

Many did also rise against his fortune, who were more hot in envying him than able to follow him, detracting his praises, disgracing his services and plotting his danger.

But Cecil's enemies on the Council had reckoned without the Queen. When Cecil's fellow councillors tried to denounce him as an evil adviser, Elizabeth flew to his defence, even castigating Leicester to his face. Clearly while Elizabeth ruled Cecil was safe.

In frustration at having failed to dislodge Cecil, Norfolk and his supporters now turned to the matter of the Duke's marriage to Mary Stuart. In the north, the Earls of Northumberland and Westmorland hoped to restore Roman Catholicism to England by overthrowing Elizabeth and replacing her with Mary Stuart, who would marry the Duke of Norfolk. To bring this about the Duke of Alva would invade England with a Spanish army from the Netherlands. Meanwhile, Mary Stuart was plotting independently to free herself and marry Norfolk. Privately they exchanged letters. It was Norfolk's tragedy that his name became linked with the Northern Revolt, for he was not a party to the planning that lay behind it.

With so many rumours surrounding Norfolk, Elizabeth began to mistrust him. Meeting him at Richmond she asked him what news he could tell her of a marriage. He shakily replied that he knew of no marriage. It seemed that Elizabeth's fears were confirmed and she ordered Norfolk "to deal no more with the Scottish cause". Norfolk was racked with self-pity. He wrote to Cecil,

I am right sorry that no man can keep me company without offence. I never deserved to be so ill thought of. I hope time will bring Her Majesty to like of them which wish best to herself and till then I must bear all with patience.

Elizabeth was anxious for her own safety and began to make plans to withstand a revolt. First she summoned Norfolk to attend her at Windsor. When he replied that he was too ill to move, Elizabeth was sure that he had joined the Northern Earls in a general rising against her.

. . . all the whole court hung in suspense and fear lest Norfolk should break forth into rebellion; and it was determined if he did so, forthwith to put the Queen of Scots to death.

Everywhere it was expected that Thomas

would take the lead in a general revolt aimed to restore Catholicism, free Mary Stuart and overthrow Elizabeth's "evil advisers". But instead of seizing his opportunity, Thomas panicked and wrote to the Earl of Westmorland, trying to stop the Northern Revolt. Westmorland's wife commented,

What a simple man the Duke is to begin a matter and not to go through with it.

Elizabeth again summoned Norfolk to Windsor "on his allegiance" and when he failed to stir he was arrested and imprisoned for 11 months in the Tower. The Northern Revolt was crushed and Northumberland and Westmorland executed.

Norfolk learned nothing from this experience and on his release he came increasingly under the influence of Roberto Ridolfi, who planned that a Spanish force would invade England and restore the country to Catholicism, while Norfolk meanwhile married Mary Stuart and took the throne. The plan was simply fantastic and reveals how far Norfolk had slipped away from reality. He wrote to Ridolfi in March 1571,

You will explain, as well to the Pope as to the Catholic King, the miserable plight in which this island is . . . I am not actuated so much by the desire to advance myself by marriage with the Queen of Scotland as by the hope of uniting all this island under a lawful Prince, and re-establishing the ancient laws and the true Christian and Catholic religion.

Norfolk instructed Ridolfi to ask Philip of Spain for troops and a general to command them. Meanwhile he would rescue Mary Stuart himself.

I am resolved, in conjunction with the forces of my friends, to hazard a battle; and essay to rescue her here by force, and at the same time to possess myself of the person of the Queen of England by way of a pawn for that of the Queen of Scotland . . . .

Once the plot was broken by Walsingham's agents it was obvious that Norfolk was guilty of treason. Tried before his peers, Norfolk was found guilty and condemned to death. Elizabeth found it difficult to condemn so prominent a nobleman but eventually Cecil pressed her to sign the warrant and Norfolk was executed.

The adverse party must needs increase when they see justice forbear against the principal, and him spared to set up the mark.

Thomas Howard lacked the qualities which had made his ancestors so successful. He was a vain, weak man, easily manipulated by unscrupulous advisers, of whose deeper motives he was unaware. He frequently acted from pique, or fear, or jealousy of Elizabeth's "new men" like Cecil and Dudley, chosen for ability or closeness to the Queen.

Robert Devereux, Earl of Essex (1567-1601)

In describing the fall of Robert Devereux in 1601, Francis Bacon compared him to the mythological Icarus, who flew too near the sun and was burned. To his contemporaries the analogy was clear. The sun was Elizabeth and Essex had presumed too far on what was in reality a shallow relationship between two selfish people; one a young and handsome favourite, the other the old and failing Queen. Essex hoped to gain political as well as financial advantages from the relationship, but Elizabeth seemed merely infatuated with a

15 Robert Devereaux, Earl of Essex, son of Lettice Knollys and stepson of Robert Dudley. His handsome appearance attracted the ageing Queen who found his flattery pleasing.

16 Lettice Knollys, Countess of Essex, who married the Queen's favourite secretly in 1579 and so incurred Elizabeth's wrath.

young man who relieved her thoughts of old age and approaching death; he was useful as a lovely toy but otherwise empty of real significance. This was Essex's tragedy. He felt that Elizabeth should have involved him in the important political decisions like that of the succession, but for advice she was always more ready to turn to his enemies Burghley and young Robert Cecil.

As the son of Lettice Knollys, Robert was a distant cousin of the Queen and, on his mother's remarriage to Leicester, Robert Dudley's step-son. Educated at Cambridge under Whitgift, Robert was an able scholar but it was clear that his future would be as a courtier. The ageing Leicester brought him to court in 1584 probably to counter the Queen's new favourite, Ralegh. In 1585 he went with Leicester to the Netherlands and fought at Zutphen. On his return he was appointed as the Queen's Master of Horse. His star was rising.

When she is abroad, nobody near her but My Lord of Essex and, at night, my Lord is at cards, or one game or another with her, that he comes not to his lodgings till birds sing in the morning.

At Tilbury in the year of the Armada Essex paraded 50 arquebusiers and 200 light horsemen in the tangerine and white colours of the Devereux family. This must have nearly bankrupted him but he felt that the display and its effect on Elizabeth was more than worth the financial risk. Elizabeth was impressed and Robert was awarded the Order of the Garter when his step-father died.

Robert's relationship with Elizabeth was stormier even than Leicester's had been. He sailed to Lisbon with Drake and Norris in 1589 even though the Queen had forbidden it. Though she showed public anger Elizabeth was pleased when he came back safely. She flattered him with gifts and the impecunious Essex benefited from the monopoly of sweet wines, which allowed him to farm import duties on wine, as Leicester once had.

As a young man of action, Essex pined for military command. Leading an English force in France, he cut a splendid figure:

As to the person of the said Earl of Essex . . . nothing more magnificent could possibly be seen: for at his entry into Compiegne he had before him six pages mounted on chargers and dressed in orange velvet all embroidered in gold. And he himself had a military cloak of orange velvet all covered in jewels . . . . His dress and the furniture on his horse alone were worth sixty thousand crowns.

Command went to Robert's head and he disobeyed Elizabeth by knighting 12 men in the field. She was furious and recalled him in a rage. In his absence he found that he had lost influence to such rising favourites as Ralegh

and Robert Cecil. Determined to build a power base to rival that of Lord Burghley he built up a faction at Essex House, which included the Bacon brothers. In 1593 Essex became a Privy Councillor and determined to play a prominent part in political decisions, notably in the question of who should succeed Elizabeth.

In 1596 Essex joined a galaxy of Elizabethan favourites including Ralegh, de Vere and Lord Howard in an attack on Cadiz. This was the greatest expedition of the Elizabethan age, yet, though the city was sacked and looted, the profits were disappointing. Essex was frustrated at his cool reception by the Queen.

17 The English raid on Cadiz in 1596 was the greatest expedition of the Elizabethan age. Led by Essex, Ralegh and Howard, the fleet achieved complete surprise, but failed to exploit their success.

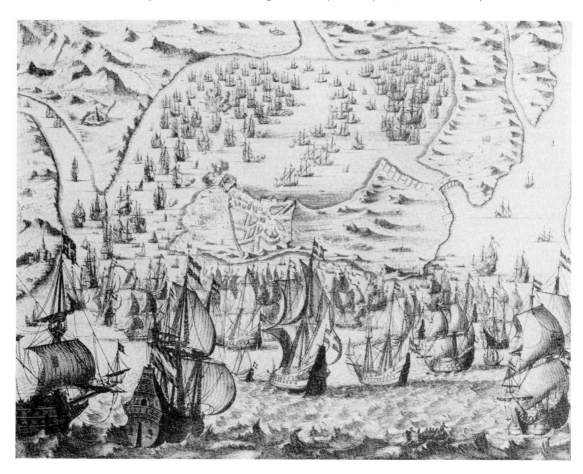

I see the fruits of these kinds of employments and . . . am much distasted with the glorious greatness of a favourite as I was before with the supposed happiness of a courtier . . . "Vanity of vanities, all is vanity".

But Elizabeth found it difficult to be angry for long with Essex and in the same year he was appointed Earl Marshal of England.

Some historians believe that Essex's erratic behaviour may have resulted from untreated syphilis but whatever the cause, Essex was about to lose his hold on the Queen. Elizabeth's views on marriage were quite clear by the 1590s and she viewed her maids-of-honour with the eye of a possessive old maid. When Essex helped the young Earl of Southampton to marry one of her maids secretly, Elizabeth was furious. A terrible row broke out between them. Essex called his Queen "a crooked old carcase" and when she hit him on the side of the head he furiously tried to draw his sword. Only the intervention of Lord Howard prevented an unprecedented incident. When Lord Keeper Egerton warned him to try to conquer himself, Essex, far from being repentant, replied

What, cannot Princes err? Cannot subjects receive wrong? Is an earthly power or authority infinite? Pardon me, pardon me, my good lord, I can never subscribe to these principles.

Even to the Queen herself he was not prepared to admit he was wrong.

When I remember that your Majesty has, by the intolerable wrong you had done both me and yourself, not only broken all laws of affection, but done against the honour of your sex . . . I cannot think your mind so dishonourable but that you punish yourself for it . . . .

For his crime Essex should have lost his head, yet again Elizabeth softened her heart towards him. But Essex was foolish not to read the signs that he was presuming too far on their friendship. This was to be the last time that Elizabeth allowed him to take such liberties.

In 1598 he was sent to Ireland as Lord-Lieutenant with the best English army ever sent there, to suppress the revolt of Tyrone. Elizabeth was furious when he failed to invade Ulster.

If sickness in the army be the reason, why was not the action undertaken when the army was in a better state? If winter's approach, why were the summer months of July and August lost? If the spring were too soon, and the summer that followed otherwise spent, if the harvest that succeeded were so neglected as nothing hath been done, then surely we must conclude that none of the four quarters of the year will be in season for you.

Ashamed by such criticism, Essex arranged a truce with the rebels and rushed back to England, storming into the Queen's bedroom at Nonsuch and demanding to be heard.

On Michaelmas eve, about ten o'clock in the morning, my lord of Essex lighted at court gate in post, and made all haste up to the presence, and so to the privy chamber, and staid not until he came to the Queen's bedchamber, where he found the Queen newly up, her hair about her face; he kneeled unto her, kissed her hands, which seemed to give him great contentment . . . . 'Tis much wondered at here that he went so boldly to her Majesty's presence, she not being ready and he so full of dirt and mire . . . .

This was the end. Elizabeth ordered him away and never saw him again. He had presumed that his influence was indispensable but Elizabeth knew she had greater need of quieter, more balanced politicians like Robert Cecil.

Essex was banished from court and this meant political and financial ruin. In Harington's opinion this affected Essex's mind:

. . . ambition thwarted in its career doth speedily lead on to madness. His speeches of the Queen becometh no man who had a sound mind . . . .

In 1601 he desperately plotted with a group of friends to overthrow Robert Cecil but he needed the support of the London populace. To incite the mob, a special performance of Shakespeare's *Richard II* was given at the Globe Theatre, including the scene in which a king is deposed. Government agents informed the Queen and the Privy Council ordered Robert's arrest. Instead, Essex and his friends rode through the London streets calling out that Ralegh was plotting against Essex's life. But royal troops blocked their way and the London mob failed to rise in his favour. Essex was arrested and tried for treason at Westminster Hall. Even his friend Francis Bacon deserted him and spoke for the prosecution. At his trial Robert Cecil spoke powerfully against him.

For wit I give you the preeminence – you have it

abundantly. For nobility also I give you place . . . I am no swordsman – there also you have the odds; but I have innocence, conscience, truth and honesty to defend me . . . in this Court I stand as an upright man, and your lordship as a delinquent . . . you have a wolf's head in a sheep's garment . . . .

In the Tower Essex made a full confession and died, after three strokes of the axe, a once popular but always impulsive man, who had won the hearts of both the people and their Queen. But he had presumed too far and had got closer to the Queen than even Leicester had dared do. And even in old age Elizabeth was not content to be mastered by any man, however handsome, courageous and charming he might be.

Gamaliel Ratsey (c.1578-1605)

Gamaliel Ratsey may seem an unusual companion for men like Leicester and Essex, yet in his own way he was the embodiment of Elizabethan values, of adventure, free enterprise and challenge to the existing system. He was a rogue-hero, the Robin Hood of Elizabeth's reign, who robbed the rich "caterpillars of the realm" yet did no harm to the poor and oppressed. And he did this without ever losing his sense of fun. The simple folk of Elizabethan England identified with his outrageous disregard for authority, following his exploits with avid interest and sorrowing at his inevitable end on the gallows.

During the sixteenth century the population of England rose by 40 per cent to nearly four million. However, there was no equivalent increase in employment and so poverty for many was inevitable. Elizabethan writers noted that more and more soldiers were joining the ranks of the poor. From the 1560s English armies were no longer based on feudal levies and were made up instead of men

taken from the poor and criminal classes. Returning home after foreign service these men simply took to the roads as "sturdy beggars" or highwaymen.

To combat these threats to law and order Elizabeth's central government depended at local level on Justices of the Peace and constables. These men were often pitifully inadequate and it is not surprising that enterprising villains like Gamaliel Ratsey were able to run rings round them. Here Shakespeare describes two such constables.

Dogberry: You are thought to be the most senseless and fit man for the constable of the watch; therefore bear you the lantern. This is your charge: You shall comprehend all vagrant men: you are to bid any man stand in the prince's name.
Second Watchman: How if he will not stand?
Dogberry: Why then, take no note of him, but let him go; and presently call the rest of the watch together, and thank God you are rid of a knave.

The Justices of the Peace were scarcely more effective. Edward Hext, a JP himself, tells how they could be overawed by a determined villain:

And they [the criminals] grow the more dangerous in that they find they have bred that fear in Justices and other inferior officers that no man dares to call them into question . . . at a recent Sessions, a tall man, a very sturdy and ancient traveller was committed by a Justice . . . to be whipped . . . he presently at the bar in the face and hearing of the whole bench, swore a great oath that if he were whipped it would be the dearest whipping for some that ever was. It struck such a fear in him that committed him that he prayed he might be deferred until the Assizes where he was delivered without any whipping or other harm. And the Justice was glad he had so pacified his wrath.

Gamaliel Ratsey was born some time in the late 1570s in Market Deeping in Lincolnshire, of a good family. His father was,

. . . enriched as well in the virtues of his wife as in the qualities of his own condition . . . but more fortunate in the love of his neighbours than in the comfort of his children.

Gamaliel was first tutored to be a scholar but,

. . . he grew less duteous and more desirous to range abroad, and see strange countries, holding his hopes frustrated and himself disparaged by living at home.

Gamaliel soon ran away to war, fighting with the English army in Ireland under the Earl of Essex. He earned promotion to Sergeant in 1601, before returning to Lincolnshire.

It was an unsettled time and unemployment was common. Many men roamed the countryside more or less involved in criminal activities. But the law was heavily enforced against such rogues and vagabonds. William Lambarde noted,

. . . many young people, not altogether evil at the first, beholding the ease and impunity that these wanderers enjoy, do abandon their honest labours . . . and do join themselves to this idle and loitering company.

Gamaliel, seeking an outlet for his restless spirit, won the confidence of a maid and her mistress in a tavern in Spalding. From here he began his career of crime by tricking a farmer out of his money and burying it near his home at Market Deeping. Arrested for the crime, he escaped "in his shirt" and was chased towards the River Welland, swimming across and heading for London.

He was a wanted man and faced the death penalty if caught. From now on he was willing to take any risk, stealing horses on the way south and joining two other desperadoes, one named Shorthose and the other Snell, who was

. . . a villain twice burned in the hand at Newgate for his bad conditions.

18 Elizabeth pickpockets or "cutpurses" were a common feature of city life and particularly of theatre audiences.

Gamaliel and his colleagues became highwaymen, preying on traffic in the area south of Peterborough, and using bluff rather than violence to achieve their ends.

On one occasion, meeting a grazier riding into Lincolnshire to buy cattle, Ratsey noticed the man was armed with a pair of pistols. First he befriended the man, then urged him to shoot with one pistol at a rabbit. When the man missed Ratsey asked to borrow the other pistol so he could shoot at the rabbit himself, only to turn on the grazier and rob him at gunpoint.

Ratsey was a master of disguise, necessary in his case as he was one of the ugliest men about. Using masks or swift changes of clothes, he sometimes rode as a merchant with Snell and Shorthose as his servants, and even dressed as an aristocrat to gain entrance to fine houses.

In the absence of a national police force Ratsey was able to escape capture for a long time yet his fate was inevitable. We do not know why he eventually came to London and resorted to petty crime but perhaps his career as a highwayman was becoming difficult. He was not a man of violence and as travellers increasingly armed themselves his tricks began to wear thin. Near Bedford one robbery went badly wrong and Ratsey was wounded by

19 "An upright man and the counterfeit crank" from *The Groundworke of Conny-catching*. The rise in population in Elizabethan England gave rise to largescale unemployment which led to an increase in casual crime. A whole literature developed to describe the different kinds of criminals one might meet on the road.

20 Whipping vagrants through the streets. The Elizabethans were alarmed by the increase in the number of rogues and vagabonds and introduced harsh laws to combat them.

21 Ale-houses became the centre of much crime. From inn keepers, highwaymen like Gamaliel Ratsey would learn of travelling parties and later waylay them on the lonely roads.

a gentleman "known to be stout and valiant". Only when Snell stabbed him in the leg was the gentleman overcome and the three robbers fled south to Southwark where they divided their spoils. Snell, however, was arrested in Duck Lane and turned state's evidence to try to save himself. Through his evidence Ratsey was arrested near Doctor's Common and taken to Newgate. Even now Ratsey was not beaten. Using acid he cut through his leg irons and nearly escaped. In court after he was condemned to the gallows, he fought off 12 men before being overcome.

Playing for time on execution day, Ratsey spied a threatening storm and asked for a delay to the execution. He also asked,

. . . that I might see the others die before me, especially the villain Snell who betrayed me.

He died, it was noted, without making any confession or expressing any regret.

Many legends surround his career but like other anti-heroes the truth was less important than the effect his adventures had on the common people. His success, however short-lived, encouraged many at a time of extreme economic hardship, while the governing classes were alarmed by his apparent success in defying the forces of law and order.

THE TURMOIL OF RELIGION

During the Reformation England's religion had been changed during successive reigns. Under Protestant Edward VI Catholics had been burned for their beliefs, while under his sister Mary, Protestants had suffered a similar fate. Elizabeth wanted to find a compromise formula, so that men and women could conform publicly to the Protestant Prayer Book and attend church, without "making a window" into their inner beliefs. The religious settlement of 1559 aimed to create a church wide enough to contain moderate Catholics and Protestants, provided that they accepted Elizabeth as head of the church in England. But extremist Protestants like Thomas Cartwright, later known as Puritans, wanted Elizabeth to go further in stamping out Catholic ritual and the authority of bishops.

Meanwhile, for Catholics there was the problem of divided loyalty. Most Catholics outwardly conformed by attending church, but others refused and paid fines as recusants. When Elizabeth was excommunicated by the Pope in 1570, England's Catholics found support for the Pope was treason against their Queen. When Catholic missionary activity began after 1580, the Privy Council took extreme measures against Catholic priests, executing Campion, not for his beliefs but because he was a political threat. The danger of French and Spanish support for Mary Stuart as a rival to Elizabeth meant that "Catholic" and "traitor" came to mean the same thing until the end of Elizabeth's reign.

Mary, Queen of Scots (1542-87)

The problem of Mary Stuart dominated the central part of Elizabeth's reign, uniting three strands of debate: the question of who should succeed Elizabeth; who, if anyone, the English Queen should marry; and lastly whether Roman Catholicism should be restored in England.

Born in 1542, Mary Stuart became Queen of Scotland at the age of six, a few days after her father's death. Henry VIII of England had wanted the young Scots queen to marry his son Edward but instead the Scottish Parliament arranged her marriage to the sickly Dauphin of France, Francis, who briefly succeed to the French throne in 1559. For a while it seemed Scotland might be drawn completely within the French sphere of influence, until the Scottish Protestant Lords of the Congregation called on young Queen Elizabeth of England to help them drive the French out of Scotland. When her husband died, the widowed Mary Stuart returned to a Scotland now much-changed, with French influence gone and the Protestant Reformation under John Knox in full swing.

Mary, half-French by blood and wholly French in upbringing, regretted the need to return to her homeland. She felt more at home at the French court and was a devoted Catholic. In addition to being the Queen of

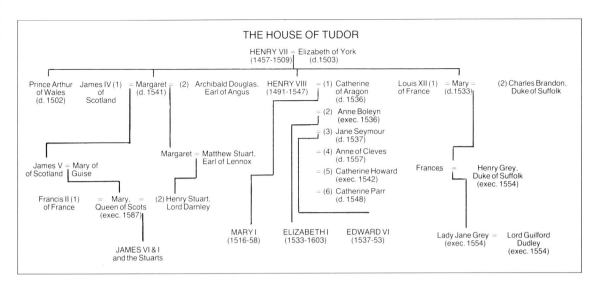

THE HOUSE OF TUDOR

HENRY VII = Elizabeth of York
(1457-1509) | (d.1503)

Prince Arthur of Wales (d. 1502) — James IV (1) of Scotland = Margaret (d. 1541) = (2) Archibald Douglas. Earl of Angus — HENRY VIII (1491-1547) = (1) Catherine of Aragon (d. 1536) — Louis XII (1) of France = Mary (d.1533) = (2) Charles Brandon. Duke of Suffolk

= (2) Anne Boleyn (exec. 1536)

= (3) Jane Seymour (d. 1537)

= (4) Anne of Cleves (d. 1557)

= (5) Catherine Howard (exec. 1542)

= (6) Catherine Parr (d. 1548)

Margaret = Matthew Stuart, Earl of Lennox

James V = Mary of of Scotland | Guise

Francis II (1) of France = Mary, Queen of Scots (exec. 1587) = (2) Henry Stuart, Lord Darnley

Frances = Henry Grey, Duke of Suffolk (exec. 1554)

MARY I (1516-58)   ELIZABETH I (1533-1603)   EDWARD VI (1537-53)

Lady Jane Grey (exec. 1554) = Lord Guilford Dudley (exec. 1554)

JAMES VI & I and the Stuarts

22 The house of Tudor, showing the Stuart claim to the English throne.

PRIMA QVOAD VIXIT COL SCOT PARENS ET FVND.

23 Mary Stuart, Queen of Scotland.

Scotland, she was also a direct descendant of Henry VII of England's daughter, Margaret, which made her the leading Catholic claimant to the English throne. Elizabeth had been declared a bastard by her own father and was regarded as illegitimate by most Catholics. Yet Mary was not her own mistress and increasingly became a pawn in international diplomacy. Throckmorton, Elizabeth's ambassador in France, wrote to her council:

Now that death has thus disposed of the late French king, whereby the Scottish queen is left a widow, one of the special things your lordships have to consider . . . is the marriage of that queen.

Elizabeth suggested her own favourite Robert Dudley as a husband but Mary impetuously chose Lord Darnley. What began as a love-match soon ended in hatred, when the jealous Darnley murdered Mary's Italian secretary, David Rizzio. Mary never forgave him and although she bore him a son, the future James VI, she soon found a new lover in the Earl of Bothwell. Mary seemed to be implicated in Darnley's mysterious death at Kirk o' Field and when she married Bothwell, she was denounced as immoral by the Scottish Kirk. How guilty Mary was is difficult for us to know. One contemporary writer thought Bothwell had forced Mary into marrying him:

24 A miniature of Bothwell – the only known portrait of him.

The Queen could not but marry him, seeing he had ravished her and laid with her against her will.

Whatever the truth, Mary was forced to abdicate in favour of her baby son in 1567. Imprisoned at Lochleven she escaped to England in 1568 and asked Elizabeth for help.

Elizabeth faced a difficult choice. She might have preferred to send Mary back to Scotland but that would have meant her certain death. On the other hand, to allow her to seek help in France or Spain might have led to an overthrow of Protestantism in Scotland and a new threat to England from the North. In the end, Elizabeth chose to keep her imprisoned in England for 19 years.

When Elizabeth was excommunicated by the Pope in 1570, this made Mary her natural replacement in the eyes of Europe's Catholics. In the first few years of her imprisonment Mary was the subject of a series of plots, in some of which she was directly involved, while in others agents acted with the intention of placing her on the English throne in order to restore the Catholic religion. After the Ridolfi Plot, many Englishmen pressed Elizabeth to execute Mary. Parliament judged that she

. . . has practised . . . to procure new rebellion to be raised within this realm. And for that intent she made choice of one Ridolphi, a merchant of Italy, who solicited the said wicked enterprises to the Pope and other . . . confederates beyond the Seas.

. . . the said Mary shall be deemed . . . a traitor.

But Elizabeth refused to harm Mary, hating to execute a fellow-sovereign. During the next decade Mary was the target for Spanish and French Catholic diplomatic activity, most of it hostile to Elizabeth. Yet the English queen found it hard to act against her "sister", knowing that she was next in line to her own throne.

Had Mary died naturally the problem of what to do with her would have solved itself. The conditions in which she was kept were often cold, damp and unhealthy, and many of her letters to Elizabeth are pitiful and show how dull was her existence. In this one she asked for poodles to be sent from France.

. . . for except in reading and writing, I take pleasure in all the little animals I can obtain . . . it is an amusement for a prisoner.

Ministers like Burghley and Walsingham regarded Mary not so much as a person as an inconvenient political reality. She was a threat while she lived, offering the Queen's enemies an alternative to Elizabeth and making an attempt on the Queen's life a way of achieving their ends. In 1584 the arrest of Francis Throckmorton revealed Mary's intrigues with the Duke of Guise. Publicly the aim was to free Mary and win toleration for English Catholics,

. . . but the intention, the bottom whereof should not at the first be made known to all men, should be, upon the Queen's Majesty's resistances, to remove her Majesty from her crown and state.

After the assassination of William of Orange in 1584, Elizabeth's loyal subjects, determined to show her enemies that they would not benefit from her death, signed the Bond of

Association, promising to pursue to the death anyone who threatened the Queen's life.

Mary's most implacable opponent was Elizabeth's Principal Secretary, the Puritan Sir Francis Walsingham, who was determined to trap her in her plotting. In July 1586, Anthony Babington was persuaded by the Jesuit priest John Ballard, that on the death of Elizabeth and the release of Mary, 60,000 Spanish soldiers were prepared to cross the Channel and restore Catholicism to England. Babington wrote to Mary:

Myself, with ten gentlemen and 100 of our followers, will undertake the delivery of your royal person from the hands of your enemies. For the dispatch of the usurper (from the obedience of whom we are by the excommunication of her made free) there be six noble gentlemen, all my private friends, who, for the zeal they have to the Catholic cause and Your Majesty's service, will undertake that tragical execution.

By tapping her correspondence with Babington, Walsingham was able to show Elizabeth incontrovertible proof that Mary not only plotted to escape, but to kill her and take the throne of England. On 17 July 1586, Mary wrote to Babington,

Everything being prepared, and the forces as well within as without . . . then you must set the six gentlemen to work and give order that, their design accomplished, I may be in some way got away from here and that all your forces shall be simultaneously in the field to receive me while we await foreign assistance . . . .

Mary had condemned herself by agreeing to the Queen's murder. Elizabeth, now convinced, wrote to her,

You have, in various ways and manners, attempted to take my life, and to bring my kingdom to destruction by bloodshed. I have never proceeded so harshly against you, but have, on the contrary, protected and maintained you like myself. These treasons will be proved to you and all made manifest.

Mary was tried for her life and found guilty, yet even now Elizabeth found it unbearably hard to condemn her rival to death. She even asked Mary's keeper, Sir Amyas Paulet, if under the Bond of Association he could arrange her death secretly. Paulet was shocked and replied,

I am so unhappy to have lived to see this unhappy day in which I am required by my most gracious sovereign to do an act which God and the law forbids . . . God forbid that I should make so foul a shipwreck of my conscience, or leave so great a blot on my posterity, to shed blood without law or warrant.

Frustrated, Elizabeth bemoaned her fate

Among the thousands who profess to be attached to me as a sovereign, not one will spare me the painful task of dipping my hands in the blood of a sister queen.

Pressed by Burghley, Elizabeth finally signed the warrant of execution, which she gave to Secretary Davison, though without telling him to forward it to Paulet at Fotheringay Castle. Secure in the knowledge that he was acting in the national interest and with the backing of the Privy Council, Davison forwarded the warrant.

Mary died with courage and dignity. The first axe blow only stunned her but the second severed her head completely. Only when the head was lifted was it discovered that the red hair of which she had been so proud was a wig, beneath which her hair was close-cropped and prematurely grey.

However, when she heard the news that Mary had been executed, Elizabeth seemed to lose her reason. She imprisoned Davison in the Tower, threatening to hang him, and ordered Lord Burghley to leave court in disgrace.

[Elizabeth's] countenance altered, her speech faltered and failed her and, through excessive sorrow, she stood in a manner astonished, insomuch that she gave herself over to passionate grief, putting herself into a mourning

habit and shedding abundance of tears . . . .

How much of this anger and sorrow was for diplomatic effect we will never know. Eventually, Davison was freed and Burghley pardoned. Mary's son, King James VI of Scotland, protested at his mother's execution, but had no intention of harming his claims to the English throne by protesting too much.

Elizabeth summed up her feelings for Mary Stuart in these lines of poetry,

The Daughter of Debate, that discord aye doth
sow,
Shall reap no gain where former rule still peace
hath taught to know.
No foreign banished wight shall anchor in this
port;
Our realm brooks not seditious sects, let them
elsewhere resort.

25 After 19 years' imprisonment in England, Mary was executed in the great hall of Fotheringay Castle.

Thomas Cartwright (1535-1603)

The Religious Settlement in 1559 did not satisfy Elizabeth's extreme Protestant supporters. They hoped for a spiritual reformation which would sweep away the rituals and superstitions of Roman Catholicism and purify the Church. By 1570 some of these "Puritans", as they became known, had gone even further and challenged the whole system of archbishops, bishops and archdeacons on which the Anglican Church depended. A Cambridge theologian, Thomas Cartwright said that his studies of the Acts of the Apostles convinced him that there was no justification for the ecclesiastical hierarchy of the Anglican Church, and that Elizabeth should turn back to the system of the early Christian church, with its committees of elders, called Presbyters, who were elected by the congregation. The Dean of York warned Lord Burghley of where these Puritan claims were leading.

At the beginning it was but a cap, a surplice . . . now it has grown to bishops, archbishops . . . to the overthrow of established order . . . . These men would not only have an equality of all ministers but would deprive the Queen of her authority and give it to the people, that every parish should choose their own minister . . . some would have a papist, others the best companion at table, not the best preacher in the pulpit . . . .

Thomas Cartwright received his education at Clare College, Cambridge, where he became a convinced Protestant. During the reign of Queen Mary, Thomas abandoned his religious teaching for the law but on the accession of Elizabeth he returned to Cambridge as a fellow of St John's College,

26 Thomas Cartwright was the most learned of the Puritan divines and one of the leaders of the Presbyterian movement.

earning a reputation for extremism and urging members of the college not to wear surplices in chapel in defiance of the 1559 Settlement. From 1569, as Professor of Divinity, his criticisms of Anglicanism were fundamental. He wanted the name and office of archbishop to be abolished, while bishops would retain purely spiritual authority, having no say in the government of the church. Like the Calvinist model, this function was to be left to the minister and presbytery of each church and congregation, the minister only holding that office after having been selected by the congregation.

But it must be remembered that civil magistrates must govern it according to the rules of God prescribed in his word, and that as they are nurses so they be servants unto the church, and as they rule the church, so they must remember to subject themselves unto the church, to submit their sceptres, to throw down their crowns before the church . . . .

Elizabeth was shocked by this attack on her royal supremacy over the Church. Archbishops Parker of Canterbury and Grindal of York, called for action against this dangerous man and the counter-attack was led by the Cambridge Vice-Chancellor, John Whitgift, who noted that Cartwright's words

. . . contain the overthrow of the prince's authority both in ecclesiastical and civil matters . . . .

Whitgift petitioned the Chancellor of the university, Lord Burghley, for Cartwright's dismissal but Cartwright's many supporters presented counter-petitions in his favour. For three months the battle raged but eventually Whitgift got his way and Cartwright was deprived of his Professorship. He went into exile at Geneva, with his friend Walter Travers, meeting there the Calvinist leader, Beza, and witnessing a Presbyterian church system in operation.

Meanwhile, other Puritans had tried to use Parliament to make changes to the religious settlement of 1559. They produced a bill to abolish the surplice, kneeling at Communion and many other popish ceremonies. But they failed, and the imprisonment of William Strickland, after his attempt to introduce a bill to reform the Book of Common Prayer, forced them to resort to a literary campaign instead. Elizabeth was not prepared to compromise and insisted that her bishops enforce conformity on her church. When the *First Admonition to Parliament* was written by John Field and Thomas Wilcox, advocating a Presbyterian system, it earned its authors a year's imprisonment. In 1572 Cartwright wrote the *Second Admonition to Parliament*, in which he proposed to

Appoint to every congregation a learned and diligent preacher. Remove homilies, articles, injunctions . . . . Take away the lordship, the loitering, the pomp, the idleness, and livings of bishops.

Again Whitgift took up the challenge from Cartwright and a literary battle began in which neither side showed the slightest toleration of the other. Cartwright was particularly intolerant, drawing deeply on the Old Testament, and demanding the death penalty for every "stubborn idolater, blasphemer, murderer, incestuous person and such-like". Here was Puritanism at its most extreme.

Although they could not outwardly support his stand against the Queen some of Elizabeth's own councillors sympathized with Cartwright, and in 1585, under the patronage of the Earl of Leicester, Thomas was allowed to return to beccome Master of an almshouse in Warwick. Leicester had asked Whitgift, now the Archbishop of Canterbury, to license Cartwright to preach but Whitgift refused "until he might be better persuaded of his conformity". He was right. Cartwright did not stop his attacks on the Church of England and for the next five years he and Travers led the presbyterian movement in England. Their aim was to agree a programme for the movement and put it into practice secretly under cover of the Church of England, even without Parliament's approval. Cartwright wrote,

That if the civil Magistrate . . . shall refuse to admit of the desired discipline then the ministers may allure the people into it and for their own parts not only may put the same in practise but likewise use all other means for the better acceptance or establishment of it.

Fears of a great Puritan conspiracy in 1588-9 prompted Whitgift to try to suppress Presbyterianism once and for all. In 1590 Cartwright was arrested and brought before the High Commission. Whitgift hoped to prove that he was a seditious threat to the state and although he failed in this, Cartwright remained in prison for two years, before being released and allowed to go to the Channel Islands. Although not destroyed, Presbyterianism was driven underground for the rest of Elizabeth's reign. Before his death, Cartwright was allowed to return to Warwick, where he died in 1603.

Thomas Cartwright was the most learned and cultured of all the Elizabethan Puritans and his Cambridge lectures in 1570 defined the doctrine from which the Presbyterian movement would later develop.

John Whitgift (1530-1604)

In appointing John Whitgift as Archbishop of Canterbury in 1583, Elizabeth hoped to stem the spread of Puritanism throughout the country. She called him "her little black husband" indicating that she was closer to this man of the cloth (the black robes of the Calvinist divine) than to any other man, and she relied on his strong sense of church discipline.

John Whitgift, being translated to Canterbury . . . the Queen gave in charge that he should take special care to restore the discipline of the Church of England, and the uniformity in the service of God established by authority of Parliament, which, through the connivance of the prelates, the obstinacy of the Puritans and the power of some noblemen was run out of square . . . .

She was not disappointed, for Whitgift was prepared to use strong measures, including the newly reorganized Court of High Commission, to act against Puritan and Catholic non-conformists. He ordered that no minister should be allowed to hold services unless they could agree to the Three Articles of 1583:

27 John Whitgift was an outspoken opponent of Puritanism. After 1583, when he became Archbishop of Canterbury, he pursued the policy preferred by Elizabeth herself, using the Court of High Commission to restore order to the Church and drive out Puritanism and Presbyterianism.

That none be permitted to preach, read, catechize, minister the sacraments, or to execute any other ecclesiastical function . . . unless he consent and subscribe to the Articles following . . .

1 That her Majesty, under God, hath, and ought to have, the sovereignty and rule over all manner of persons born within her realms . . . either ecclesiastical or temporal, soever they be . . . .

2 That the Book of Common Prayer, and of ordering bishops, priests and deacons, containeth nothing in it contrary to the word of God . . . and that he himself will use the form of the said book prescribed in public prayer and administration of the sacraments, and none other.

3 That he alloweth the book of Articles, agreed upon by the archbishops and bishops of both provinces, and the whole clergy in the Convocation holden at London in the year of our Lord God 1562 . . . and that he believeth all the Articles therein contained to be agreeable to the word of God.

But the second article was unacceptable to most Puritans and some 300 clergymen were forced to resign. This was the very point on which Whitgift had fought Cartwright in the 1570s. The Puritans had supporters in high places, who were not happy to see ministers under their own patronage dragged before the ecclesiastical court. Under pressure from the Privy Council Whitgift changed the wording of the Articles and most of the deprived clergy were reinstated.

But Whitgift had learned from his mistake. In 1584 he issued a set of 24 questions to be enforced by the Court of High Commission by an *ex officio* oath. This time his target was the Puritan leadership, not the moderate rank and file of clergy. Priests would be asked whether they used the Book of Common Prayer without alteration, or wore the prescribed dress or omitted the sign of the cross in baptism. The priest would be required to swear that he would answer questions truthfully before he knew which questions were to be asked. This alarmed lawyers like William Cecil who claimed this procedure played no part in English common law. In 1584, he wrote to Whitgift complaining that "lewd, evil, unprofitable men and clergy" were not harmed by the articles while some "diligent, learned and zealous" ones were.

I conclude that, according to my simple judgement, this kind of proceeding is too much savouring of the Romish inquisition and is rather a device to seek for offenders than to reform any. This is not the charitable instruction that I thought was intended.

Sir Francis Knollys, too, was furious, seeing

the course of Popish treason to be neglected and to see the zealous preachers of the gospel, sound in doctrine (who are the most diligent barkers against the Popish wolf to save the fold and flock of Christ) to be persecuted and put to silence.

Puritan leaders like John Field now prepared evidence for Parliament to show that many preachers within the established church were quite unfit for their office and far worse than the Puritans questioned by the Court of High Commission. In Essex, Field reported,

Mr Bulie, parson of Borlie, a man of scandalous life, a drunkard.
Mr Philips, parson of Sturmer, sometime a Popish priest.
Mr Hall, parson of West Ham, a drunkard.
Mr Warrener, parson of West Mersey, an adulterer.

This campaign caused a sensation in Parliament and there were calls for the replacement of the 1559 Book of Common Prayer by the Geneva Prayer Book. Eventually Elizabeth summoned the Speaker of the Commons to forbid the House to debate church matters any further.

Whitgift's appointment to the Privy Council in 1586 made him the first and only Elizabethan ecclesiastic to exercise political power. Confident of the support of the Queen and of Lord Chancellor Hatton, he continued to strengthen and restore discipline in the Church. The publication of the Marprelate tracts in 1588-9, aimed at criticizing Whitgift himself, provoked him into strict counter-measures. Assisted by his chaplain, Richard Bancroft, Whitgift set about hunting down the secret press which the Puritans had been using. When it was discovered, the printers were tortured into revealing information. The next year Cartwright and ten others were arrested and brought before the Court of High Commission.

Yet Whitgift had no desire to create Puritan martyrs and once conformity had been re-established he was prepared to relax his severity. In 1595 his Lambeth Articles made concessions to Calvinist doctrines like Predestination:

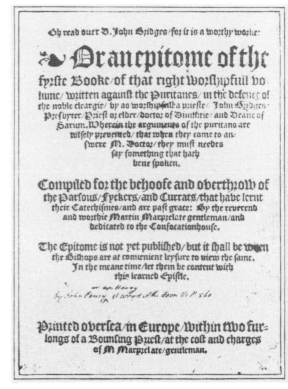

28 The title-page of one of the Marprelate Tracts of 1588-9 – annonymous Puritan pamphlets which ridiculed leading Anglican bishops, notably Archbishop Whitgift.

1 . . . God from eternity predestined certain men to life and condemned others to death.
3 . . . The number of the predestined is prescribed and certain and it cannot be increased or diminished.
4 . . . Those who are not predestined to salvation shall of necessity be damned on account of their sins.

Articles like these won the disapproval of Elizabeth herself and were held in abeyance. Robert Cecil wrote to Whitgift of Elizabeth's feelings.

. . . she mislikes much that any allowance has been given by your Grace and the rest of any points to be disputed of Predestination, being a matter tender and dangerous to weak, ignorant minds.

Yet the Queen and her Archbishop were not at odds for long. In 1603, on her deathbed,

Elizabeth turned for comfort to "her little black husband":

> . . . she would not endure any talk . . . unless it were with the Archbishop of Canterbury, with whom she often prayed with great fervency and devotion until little by little her speech failed her.

Whitgift lived for just a year longer himself, during which he took part in the Hampton Court Conference, supporting James I in his resistance to doctrinal changes but upholding calls for a new translation of the Bible.

Edmund Campion (1540-81)

From 1574 English missionary priests trained at the seminary at Douai returned to England hoping to win back their country to Catholicism. In 1580 they were joined by the Jesuits, Robert Parsons and Edmund Campion, men willing to give their lives for their faith, whose aims were spiritual, not political. As Campion said, "I am now as a dead man to this world, and willing to put my head under every man's foot." A contemporary poet wrote,

God knows it is not force nor might,
Nor war nor warlike band,
Nor shield and spear, nor dint of sword,
That must convert the land.
It is the blood of martyrs . . . .

29 Edmund Campion with Father Robert Parsons. Campion failed to understand that after Elizabeth's excommunication by the Pope in 1570, failure to acknowledge her as head of the Church of England was not a religious offence but treason.

Born in London in 1540 Edmund Campion was a precocious scholar, taking his MA at Oxford at the age of 14 and through his oratory winning the attention of both Mary and Elizabeth. Patronized by both Burghley and Leicester he was already a deacon in the Anglican Church by 1568 and destined for high office. However, at this time he underwent a spiritual crisis. Driven from Oxford for his increasingly Catholic views he fled to the continent, visiting Douai and travelling to Rome where he became a Jesuit. Edmund then became a professor at the Jesuit College in Prague.

In 1580 Campion was chosen by Pope Gregory XIII to lead the first Jesuit mission to England together with Robert Parsons. Though a very spiritual man Edmund was politically naïve. His instructions to avoid disputes with heretics, and not to challenge the position of the Queen were impossible in an England threatened by the power of Catholic Spain and the Pope.

My charge is . . . to preach the gospel, to minister the sacraments, to instruct the simple, to reform sinners . . . I am strictly forbidden by our fathers that sent me to deal in any respect with matters of state or policy of the realm . . . .

Edmund truly believed this, but Elizabeth's Puritan ministers, like Leicester, Walsingham and Burghley saw loyalty to Rome as treason against Elizabeth. Catholics in England must choose between their Queen or the Pope: there could be no middle course.

So Campion's plans were doomed from the start. Word had reached England that he was coming but although the ports were watched, he managed to evade government agents at Dover and found safe houses where loyal Catholics sheltered him. He was persuaded by friends to write a letter to the Privy Council, later known as "Campion's Bragge", giving his reasons for coming to England, to be delivered only if he was arrested. Somehow a copy fell into the hands of the Privy Council, who were alarmed by Edmund's confidence.

. . . I know perfectly that no one Protestant, nor all the Protestants living . . . can maintain their doctrine in disputation I am to sue most humbly and instantly for the combat with all and every one of them . . . .

Elizabeth's advisers hoped that Catholicism would wither away without the need for direct action. Yet as he toured England, trying to win back the governing class and intellectuals, Edmund offered a real threat of Catholic revival. Campion would have to be silenced.

Meanwhile Edmund moved secretly from one safe house to another, hearing confessions, celebrating masses, giving Communion and reclaiming lapsed believers. When government agents were near he and his companions were hidden in secret hideaways called priest holes. Robert Parsons had set up a secret printing press and Edmund's pamphlet *Ten Reasons Against the Anglican Church*, which attacked the foundations of Anglicanism, was widely circulated. Eventually a priest-hunter named Eliot hearing Campion's mass at Lyford, in Berkshire, fetched the local magistrate. Returning to the house they searched everywhere for Edmund.

David Jenkins, by God's great goodness, espied a certain secret place, which he quickly found to be hollow; and with a pin of iron . . . he forthwith did break a hole into the said place; where then presently he perceived the said Priests lying all close together on a bed, of purpose there laid for them; where they had bread, meat and drink sufficient to have relieved them three or four days together.

Taken to London, Edmund was led through the city wearing a paper hat proclaiming, "Campion the seditious Jesuit". He was sent to the "Little Ease" in the Tower, a cell so small he could neither stand nor lie down. But Edmund had influential friends who tried to save his life by persuading him to conform. He was taken before Leicester and the Queen at Leicester House and challenged to explain his *Ten Reasons*, but his answers satisfied nobody. Elizabeth herself asked if he acknowledged her as Queen. Edmund answered that she was his lawful Queen. When she asked if the Pope could excommunicate her, he replied that such political matters were beyond him. Burghley then asked him the "Bloody Question", which would trap so many future Jesuits. If a Catholic invasion of England took place whom would he support "Pope or Queen"? Realising that he was trapped, Edmund replied that he would leave the choice to God's grace.

Elizabeth knew that Edmund was no threat to her personally, only a gentle and honest priest. Yet his example was a threat to her Church. She offered him high office in the Protestant Church if he would conform but he refused. Under torture by the rack he revealed the names of the safe houses in which he had stayed.

7 Nov. 1581. After having again terribly tormented Campion . . . they have indicted him, as they call it here, as a traitor, with sixteen others, mostly clergymen . . . Campion not having yet been brought to trial, as he is all dislocated and cannot move.

At his eventual trial for treason he defended not himself, but a thousand years of English history:

The only thing that we have now to say is that, if our religion do make us traitors, then we are worthy to be condemned, but otherwise are and have been as true subjects as ever the Queen had. In condemning us, you condemn all your own ancestors, all the ancient priests, bishops and kings — all that was once the glory of England — the island of saints and the most devoted child of the See of Peter.

Edmund was sentenced to die the horrible death of a traitor at Tyburn, though it is clear that an influential person had ordered the executioner to ensure he was dead before he was disembowelled and quartered. Before he

30 and 31 Many Catholic priests suffered torture and death in Elizabeth's reign because of their refusal to acknowledge Elizabeth as head of the Church in England.

died he prayed for the Queen. A voice from the crowd called, "Which Queen?" and Edmund answered, "For Elizabeth! For your Queen and mine!" Edmund Campion died a true and loyal Englishman.

THE ELIZABETHAN RENAISSANCE

Under Elizabeth's father, Henry VIII, the English Court had been the centre of a group of politicians, painters and poets, both English and foreign, who brought the ideas of the Italian Renaissance to England. During Henry's secure reign royal and noble patronage of the arts flourished, but the religious struggles of the next two reigns cut England off from the mainstream of European ideas, which were still essentially Catholic. Elizabeth's adherence to a strong national church irrevocably severed England's continental influences and instead caused her men of letters to turn in upon England's medieval traditions. The English Renaissance was essentially a literary one, with writers like Edmund Spenser, Philip Sidney, Christopher Marlowe and others creating a golden age for English literature.

32 The Elizabethan Renaissance saw the rise of popular theatre. Here a play is performed in an inn yard.

England's greatest contribution to the period of the Renaissance was in the form of popular theatre. The growth of literacy created a well-informed population, particularly in London, and the huge expansion of the capital, from a town of some 50,000 people in 1550 to one of 250,000 by the end of Elizabeth's reign, provided an audience which was both willing and eager to attend plays. One of the many playwrights able to satisfy this demand was Christopher Marlowe and not far behind him were the younger Shakespeare and Jonson. With patronage from men like the Earl of Leicester, companies of actors were set up and the first theatrical impresarios appeared, like James Burbage, Edward Alleyn and Philip Henslowe. Pre-eminent among the early actors was Richard Burbage.

Christopher Marlowe (1564-93)

The death of Christopher Marlowe at the age of 29 is one of the mysteries of Elizabeth's reign. It is also one of the greatest losses English literature has ever suffered. How great might Marlowe have been had he lived, and could he even have overshadowed Shakespeare? The problem for Marlowe was one of personality. As a brilliant and ambitious young man, full of great ideas, the future must have seemed bright in an age where upward social mobility was possible, particularly through the good offices of a wealthy patron. But Christopher was no tame courtier. He was a tempestuous, argumentative man, frequently found in taverns and as happy in low company as with men of good breeding. To use a modern phrase, he was his own worst enemy.

Born in Kent and educated at Kings School, Canterbury and Cambridge, Christopher was a brilliant scholar. Yet his studies were overshadowed by other activities at which we can only guess. In 1587 he faced rejection for his MA degree, as he had been absent from Cambridge visiting the Catholic seminary at Rheims, set up by Cardinal William Allen. Only when the Privy Council advised the university that Christopher had been engaged on matters "touching the benefit of the country" was the degree awarded. In fact, he had been spying for Walsingham, who was worried by the number of English students going to train as Catholic priests at Rheims. Spying aside, Marlowe had also been busy writing plays and poetry at Cambridge. Dating is difficult but *Tamburlaine the Great* was probably finished before he left Cambridge in 1587 and first performed by the Lord Admiral's Men in that year, with Edward Alleyn in the leading role. The part of Tamburlaine is one of the greatest written for the Elizabethan stage, symbolizing the thirst for power of Elizabethan courtiers like Leicester, Essex, Hatton, Ralegh and many others.

What daring god torments my body thus
And seeks to conquer mighty Tamburlaine?
Shall sickness prove me now to be a man
That have been term'd "the Terror of the World"?

In 1588 Christopher moved to London to try his luck in the theatre, living by his wits and continuing to work for Walsingham's "secret service". He was popular with theatre-owners and actors and *Tamburlaine* was a great success, combining as it did an exotic story with powerful blank verse that was new to the Elizabethan theatre. In *The Jew of Malta* Marlowe caricatured the Italian statesman Machiavelli in the person of Barabas. It seems certain that this play, popular through its

The Tragicall Historie of the Life and Death of Doctor Faustus.

With new Additions.

Written by CH. MAR.

Printed at London for *Iohn Wright*, and are to be sold at his
shop without Newgate. 1631.

33 (left) This woodcut illustrates a scene from Christopher Marlowe's play *Dr Faustus*. Faustus, standing within a magical circle, is conjuring up Mephistopheles.

34 Edward Alleyn. Actors were previously classed with rogues and vagabonds, but during Elizabeth's reign, when theatre-going became popular and fashionable, writers like Marlowe and later Shakespeare provided demanding roles for a new class of actors.

appeal to Elizabethan anti-semitism, influenced Shakespeare's *Merchant of Venice* and his character Shylock.

More plays followed: *Edward II, Doctor Faustus, The Massacre of Paris*, confirming his considerable reputation, and, when the London theatres were closed by plague in 1592-3, Marlowe turned his hand to poetry, writing "Hero and Leander" to rival Shakespeare's "Venus and Adonis", and aiming to win the patronage of the Earl of Southampton. His most famous poem "The Passionate Shepherd to his Love" begins

Come live with me and be my love
And we will all the pleasures prove

That valleys, groves or hills and fields,
Woods or steepy mountain yields.

But Marlowe's success at such an early age won him enemies. Although Shakespeare admired his work, others like Robert Greene viciously attacked him. Christopher was constantly in trouble with the law, frequenting low drinking houses and often becoming involved in street brawls. In 1589 he was involved in a brawl with poet Thomas Watson and another man named William Bradley. Watson, trying to break up the fight between Marlowe and Bradley, killed the latter and the two poets were put in Newgate Prison, appearing before a judge at the Old Bailey. Marlowe was pardoned, possibly on the instructions of a higher authority for he was still involved in spying for Walsingham.

In London Marlowe shared lodgings with a fellow-dramatist Thomas Kyd. When Kyd was arrested on suspicion of writing atheistical works, he claimed under torture that Marlowe was also an atheist and had denied the divinity of Jesus Christ. Marlowe was arrested but again his lenient treatment suggests that the Privy Council found him too useful to lose.

On 30 March 1593, Marlowe went to Deptford to meet some friends at Eleanor Bull's tavern. After heavy drinking a dispute broke out over the bill and a companion named Frizer stabbed Marlowe above the eye, killing him instantly. A contemporary account of the inquest reports,

Frizer is found to have acted in defence of his own life. But though this is the Coroner's verdict, there want not other stories making his end more fearful. He is reported to have been an atheist, a blasphemer, given to the vice of sodomy; which offences with many others of a like nature had been charged against him in a paper sent to the Lord Keeper but three days before his death . . . .

And yet a mystery remains. Was Christopher simply a victim of his own evil temper or had someone in authority arranged to have him silenced?

During the brief period of six years he devoted to writing, Marlowe showed himself a worthy rival to Shakespeare. Original, powerful and lyrical, he dominated the English stage and gave a lead to Shakespeare and the Jacobeans in his observance of the psychology of great men. He stimulated the growth of drama in England and we can only lament the waste of such talent at such a young age.

Richard Burbage (1567-1619)

During the Elizabethan age theatres flourished and actors gained an air of respectability in contrast to earlier views of them as vagabonds, pedlars and rogues. It had been to escape this criticism that companies of players were set up by leading nobles like the Earl of Leicester to perform the latest plays in their great houses. The exaggerated style of acting used in

35 Richard Burbage was generally considered the greatest actor of his time and gave the first performance of many of Shakespeare's most famous roles, among them Hamlet and Richard III.

To the Reader.
This Figure, that thou here seest put,
It was for gentle Shakespeare cut;
Wherein the Grauer had a strife
with Nature, to out-doo the life:
O, could he but haue drawne his wit
As well in brasse, as he hath hit
Hisface; the Print would then surpasse
All, that was euer writ in brasse.
But, since he cannot, Reader, looke
Not on his Picture, but his Booke.
                                        B. I.

36 William Shakespeare. He was highly regarded even at the end of Elizabeth's reign when he was known as an actor as well as a writer.

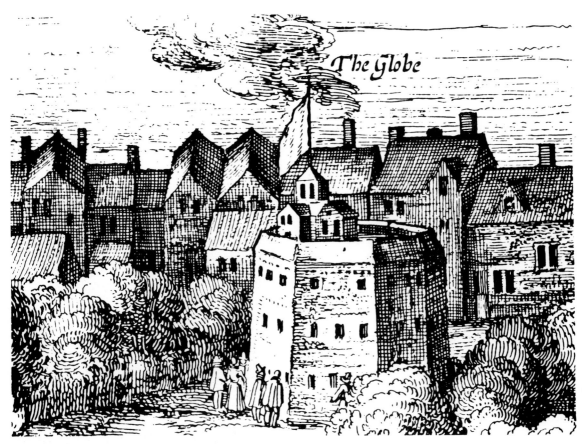

The Globe

medieval plays, in masques and mummeries began to be replaced by more naturalistic acting and it was the emergence of such great figures as Edward Alleyn, James Burbage and greatest of all, Richard Burbage, that enabled writers like Shakespeare to portray their complex characters to the public. Burbage's reputation survived his death as this comment, made in 1664, shows:

. . . he was a delightful Proteus, so wholly transforming himself into his part, and putting off himself with his clothes, as he never assumed himself again until the play was done: there being as much difference between him and one of our common actors, as between a ballad singer who only mouths it, and an excellent singer, who knows all his graces, and can artfully vary and modulate his voice, even to know how much breath he is to give every syllable.

Richard came from a theatrical family, his

37 The Globe Theatre was opened in Maiden Lane, on Bankside, in 1599. It became the most famous of London's Elizabethan theatres through its association with Shakespeare's plays.

father, James, being a famous actor and theatre-owner. His earliest appearances were in his father's Shoreditch theatre, where he clearly picked up the elements of his art. In 1587, Richard joined the Earl of Leicester's Players and stayed with them until 1603, by which time the group was known as the King's Men. From 1594 he was on very close terms with a fellow-actor and playwright, William Shakespeare, and it was with Burbage in mind that Shakespeare wrote some of his most famous roles. It was Burbage who first breathed life into the parts of Romeo and Malvolio, while the great tragic roles of Macbeth, Hamlet, Lear and Othello were also first his. But greatest of all, and certainly his most popular part, was that of the evil hunchbacked king, Richard III.

I, that am curtail'd of this fair proportion,
Cheated of feature by dissembling nature,
Deform'd, unfinish'd, sent before my time
Into this breathing world, scarce half made up,
And that so lamely and unfashionable
That dogs bark at me as I halt by them;
Why, I, in that weak piping time of peace,
Have no delight to pass away the time;
Unless to spy my shadow in the sun,
And descant on mine own deformity;
And therefore since I cannot prove a lover
To entertain these fair, well-spoken days,
I am determined to prove a villain . . . .

When James Burbage died, his sons inherited his theatres at Shoreditch and Blackfriars, as well as his dispute with Giles Allen over the lease of the Shoreditch site. To avoid trouble, Richard and his brother pulled down the latter theatre, building it again at Southwark and renaming it the Globe for its opening in 1599. It was here that supporters of the Earl of Essex persuaded Shakespeare to stage *Richard II* on the night before Essex's fateful rising in 1601. Perhaps it was Burbage who spoke the lines to remind Essex of just how high he had set his sights:

Not all the water in the rough, rude sea
Can wash the balm from an anointed king . . . .

Richard became wealthy from his acting and his theatre ownership, and he was much in demand by other playwrights, including Ben Jonson, Beaumont and Fletcher. On his death in 1618 men spoke as if acting itself had died. John Fletcher wrote,

He's gone, and with him what a world are dead,
Which he revived to be revived so,
No more young Hamlet, old Heironymoe.
King Lear, the grieved Moor, and more beside,
That lived in him, have now for ever died.
Oft have I seen him leap into the grave,
Suiting the person which he seemed to have
Of a sad lover with so true an eye,
That thee I would have sworn, he meant to die.
Oft have I seen him play this part in jest,
So lively that spectators and the rest
Of his sad crew, whilst he but seemed to bleed,
Amazed, thought even then he died in deed.

Sir Philip Sidney (1554-86)

It is said that Elizabeth I refused to help Philip Sidney whose European connections made him a strong candidate for the elective crown of Poland, because she feared "to lose the jewel of her times". And in an age which boasted such "jewels" as Shakespeare, Marlowe, Ralegh, Essex and many others, Philip Sidney stood alone as the epitome of the English Renaissance Man. He was a Protestant hero and a Christian knight, yet his death was mourned equally in Catholic as well as Protestant lands. He was seen as the embodiment of virtue and the ideal gentleman. Spenser declared, "he was second to none", while the historian Camden said, "he was the great glory of his family, the great hope of mankind, the most lively pattern of virtue and the glory of the world". Who, then, was this paragon of virtue, who died young and yet achieved so much?

Philip was born in Kent in 1554 with a number of silver spoons in his mouth. Philip II of Spain stood as his godfather, while Robert Dudley, Earl of Leicester was his uncle. He spent an idyllic childhood at Penshurst Place, in Kent, before attending Shrewsbury School and Christ Church, Oxford, where he first met Fulke Greville. He was happy in the company of a brilliant circle of friends including Camden, Campion, Hakluyt and Ralegh. In 1572 his father encouraged him to further his education by a

38 Sir Philip Sidney. A true man of the Renaissance, he was considered a flower of chivalry as well as warrior, poet, courtier and diplomat.

grand tour of Europe, where he extended his considerable knowledge of languages, meeting the foremost European statesmen. In addition to his great learning, Philip was blessed with good looks, athleticism and all the social graces. Contemporaries soon referred to him as "the flower of England".

After attending Leicester's magical celebrations for the Queen's visit to Kenilworth in 1575, he went to court as Cup Bearer to Elizabeth. Here he met Walter Devereux, who wanted him to marry his daughter Penelope, the "Stella" of Philip's later sonnets. But the young man was too much in love with the world to concentrate on any one woman. Politics became his obsession as his Protestant background prompted him to explore the possibilities of a Protestant League led by England to help the Dutch in their struggle against Spain. He met William of Orange and carried out diplomatic missions for Elizabeth. With the backing of the Earl of Leicester he wrote to Elizabeth arguing strongly against her proposed marriage to the French Duc D'Alençon. As a result he lost the Queen's favour and left court under a cloud, planning to devote himself to literature.

Philip had met Italian writers on his tour of Europe and now adopted some of their devices in his own prose and poetry. He encouraged English writers like Spenser to try to rival the achievements of the Italians and advice like this helped a number of young, aspiring writers:

Of all sciences is our poet the monarch. For he doth not only show the way, but giveth so sweet a prospect into the way, as will entice any man to enter into it. Nay, he doth, as if your journey should lie through a fair vineyard, at the first give you a cluster of grapes, that full of that taste, you may long to pass further. He beginneth not with obscure definitions, which . . . must load the memory with doubtfulness; but he cometh to you with words set in delightful proportion, either accompanied with, or prepared for, the well enchanting skill of music; and with a tale forsooth he cometh unto you, with a tale that holdeth children from play, and old men from the chimney corner.

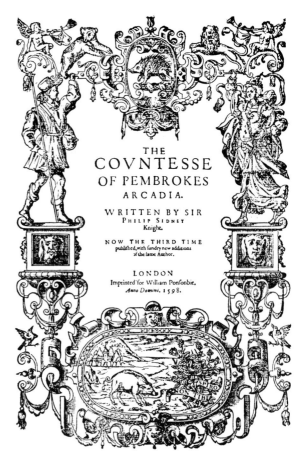

39 As a poet, Sidney's importance rests in his technical virtuosity and his experiments with classical metres and Italian verse forms. This is the title-page from his most important work, *Poems from Old Arcadia.*

In 1582 Philip fell in love with Penelope Devereux, now a married woman and beyond him. He sublimated his feelings in his "Astrophil" and "Stella" poems, written not for publication but to satisfy his own burning ardour.

Stella, think not that I by verse seek fame
Who seek, who hope, who love, who live but thee;
Thine eyes my pride, thy lips mine history:
If thou praise not, all other praise is shame.

Denied Penelope, he met and married Frances Walsingham in 1583, daughter of Elizabeth's great minister. This was an important political marriage within the Protestant circles of the government. The Queen herself was not pleased but duly knighted Philip the following year, although still denying him the diplomatic posts he merited.

When Elizabeth at last decided to send troops to help the Protestant cause in the Netherlands, Philip accompanied his uncle Leicester as Governor of the town of Flushing and a commander of the cavalry. It was at the battle of Zutphen in 1586 that the real Philip Sidney died and was replaced by the legendary "flower of chivalry". Seeing that his commander had ridden without thigh armour, Philip thought it cowardly to wear his own. After charging the Spanish lines three times he was hit by a bullet in the thigh and died later at Arnhem. His friend and biographer, Fulke Greville, left this immortal picture of the qualities of generosity by which Philip had lived and died.

In this sad progress, passing along by the rest of the army, where his uncle the General was, and being thirsty with excess of bleeding he called for drink, which was presently brought him, he saw a poor soldier carried along . . . ghastly casting up his eyes at the bottle; which Sir Philip perceiving, took it from his head before he drank, and delivered it to the poor man with these words: "Thy necessity is yet greater than mine!"

The death of Philip Sidney was mourned throughout Europe and his body lay in state at Flushing for eight days before being taken back to England where it was buried at St Paul's Cathedral, after a state funeral. The poets who owed so much to his example and his encouragement, all composed elegies on his death. Edmund Spenser wrote,

He grew up fast in goodnes and in grace,
And doubly fair wax both in mind and face.

Which daily more and more he did augment,
With gentle usage, and demeanour mild;
That all men's hearts with secret ravishment
He stole away, and wittingly beguiled.

40 Sir Philip Sidney's funeral procession. His death at the battle of Zutphen was mourned equally by Catholic and Protestant princes.

ELIZABETHAN EXPLORATION

The Elizabethan Age was the period of English "sea dogs", seaman more often outside than within the law, pirates, plunderes, explorers, traders and patriots; sometimes all of these things at the same time. Their names are better known to us today than any of Elizabeth's courtiers. If Drake, Ralegh, Grenville, Hawkins and Frobisher over-shadow Cecil, Dudley, Hatton, Knollys and Walsingham, it is because they laid the foundation for something that became fundamental to England's future – maritime and colonial power. And they were free spirits, self-made men, representing the vital energies of the period in which they lived. Richard Hakluyt, through whose advocacy and propaganda these men flourished and England grew great at sea, noted that it had not always been so. England was a century behind the Spanish and Portuguese explorers, whose example had not inspired English sailors to follow them.

But alas our English nation were either altogether destitute of such clear lights and inducements, or if they had any inkling at all, it was as misty as they found the North Seas, and so obscure and ambiguous that it was meet rather to deter them than to give them encouragement.

Yet by 1588 Hakluyt could rejoice,

For which of the kings of this land before Her Majesty had their banners ever seen in the Caspian Sea? Which of them hath ever dealt with the Emperor of Persia, as her Majesty hath done . . . . What English ships did ever anchor in the mighty river of Plate; pass and repass the unpassable (in former opinion) strait of Magellan . . . and last of all return home most richly laden with the commodities of China, as the subjects of this now flourishing monarchy have done?

Sir Martin Frobisher (1539-94)

There is one way left to discover which is unto the North. For out of Spain they had discovered all the Indies and the seas occidental, and out of Portugal all the Indies and seas oriental.

The English mariner Robert Thorne wrote this in 1527 and so began the attempts by English explorers to find a northern passage to the fabulously wealthy Indies and Cathay. The idea of a north-west passage appealed both to intellectuals like John Dee and Richard Hakluyt, and to men of action like Humphrey Gilbert and Martin Frobisher. They all remembered Cabot's voyage of 1509 when he discovered a large inlet, now Hudson's Bay, before turning back. Perhaps this had been the passage. It needed a fearless captain to lead a new expedition there to find out.

Unlike many Elizabethan mariners, Martin

WYYMPER SC

Frobisher was no "man of Devon" but a dour Yorkshireman, of good family, who spent his childhood with a wealthy relative in London. Martin was no scholar, and was noted instead for "his great spirit and bold courage and

41 Sir Martin Frobisher, unlike other Elizabethan "sea dogs" was a Yorkshireman. His three arduous journeys to the Arctic regions in search of the North-West passage failed, but his courage against the Armada won him a knighthood.

strength of body". He learned his craft on trading voyages to Guinea and as a pirate preying on Spanish ships.

For his first expedition Frobisher had just two small barques, the *Gabriel* and the *Michael*, three-masted ships of under 50 tons, and a tiny pinnace, but was equipped with the best nautical aids available, books on navigation and maps prepared by the Muscovy Company. From Greenland, Frobisher struck westwards in the *Gabriel*, reaching what he thought to be the long-sought channel, which he named Frobisher Strait. His party met Eskimos in kayaks, who proved to be hostile. His pilot, Christopher Hall, described them.

They be like Tartars with long black hair, broad faces and flat noses and tawny in colour, wearing sealskins . . . the women are marked in the face with blue streaks down the cheeks and around the eyes.

42 These drawings by John White show the Eskimo mother and baby on the left, and the Eskimo man on the right, captured by Frobisher in 1577 and brought back to England.

Having found marcasite (fool's gold) Frobisher sailed home, bringing with him a single Eskimo prisoner, whom the powerful Frobisher had lifted bodily out of his kayak into the *Gabriel*. In England the marcasite was thought to contain gold ore.

It seemed Martin's fortune was made and people flocked to sponsor a second voyage. The Cathay Company, set up by Michael Lok, appointed Martin Captain-General, and the Queen gave him the 200-ton *Aid*, and the title of Admiral of the Seas. With miners to look for gold and six criminals to be released in the new lands to civilize the natives, Frobisher sailed in 1577. This time he planned to collect ore and, if possible, sail through Frobisher Strait to Cathay.

Icebergs and pack ice proved a hazard and his men showed great courage.

To the everlasting renown of our nation . . . some, having poles, pikes, pieces of timber, and oars in their hands, stood almost day and night without any rest, bearing off the force and breaking the sway of the ice. . . .

Again the Eskimos were hostile, Frobisher being hit in the buttock by an arrow. Only

43 In 1577 Frobisher's men found the Eskimos hostile. This painting by one of his crew, John White, shows the Eskimos in their kayaks and on land firing arrows at Frobisher's men who reply with their firearms.

after firing arquebuses did the sailors drive them off. After mining 200 tons of ore and taking hostages, Martin returned again to England, to a greater triumph even than the previous year. The ore was declared rich in gold and silver, and a third voyage was planned, financed by the Queen and many of her courtiers.

With 15 ships Frobisher set out in 1578, carrying the hopes of many influential men. They were to be dashed. He brought back 1300 tons of ore, found to be quite worthless, fit only "for mending the roads" and, disturbed by "many strange meteors" in the sky, the aurora borealis, he returned without setting up the small, planned settlement. News of the voyage's failure and losses of over £20,000 bankrupted Lok, who accused Frobisher of cheating him. Shunned by his influential friends, Frobisher's fall from grace was complete. The Queen, who had recently rewarded him with a golden chain, now refused to see him or employ him again.

Martin returned to privateering and piracy.

It was not until the war with Spain in the 1580s, that the call came again to serve his Queen. He went with Drake in 1585 to attack the Spanish West Indies and during the fighting against the Armada in 1588 commanded the *Triumph*, the largest ship in the English fleet, twice driving off four Spanish galleons near Portland Bill, and being knighted for his bravery. Ever the man of action, Frobisher died at sea fighting the Spaniards in 1594.

Frobisher was a man, "who had in him not only greatness but a human quality which made men curse him and love him, grumble at him and toil for him". Though failing to find the North-West Passage, his voyages added much to the geographical knowledge of the Elizabethan Age. He was not the first to be fooled by "fool's gold" and lacking the polish of men like Gilbert and Ralegh he was not at home with courtiers and financiers. Yet of the English "sea-dogs" he was the steadiest, being simple, honest and loyal to Queen and country.

Richard Hakluyt (1552-1616)

Richard Hakluyt was born in London in 1552 and brought up by a rich lawyer cousin, who first introduced him to travel and geography.

I found . . . certain books of Cosmography, with an universal Map: he seeing me somewhat curious . . . began to instruct my ignorance . . . my cousin's discourse . . . took in me so deep an impression that I resolved . . . to read over whatsoever printed or written discoveries and voyages I found either in Greek, Latin, Italian, Spanish, Portuguese, French or English . . . .

Winning a scholarship to Oxford, Richard gained an MA in 1577 and went on to take holy orders. Unusually, this did not bar him from mixing with seamen and explorers like

Humphrey Gilbert, Francis Drake and Martin Frobisher, as well as Dr John Dee and cosmographers like Abraham Ortelius and Gerardus Mercator. He also began collecting globes, maps and nautical instruments of every kind and possibly gave the first ever geography lectures at Oxford University.

He soon became an advocate of English exploration overseas. In his *Discourse on the Strait of Magellan* he supported the search for the North-West Passage, aiming to open a new market for English wool and hoping to establish a colony in the Spice Islands. In 1580, in his *Divers Voyages to America* Richard argued that the explorations of the Cabots should have encouraged the English to set up settlements in North America.

THE
PRINCIPAL NAVI-
GATIONS, VOIAGES,
TRAFFIQVES AND DISCO-
ueries of the English Nation, made by Sea
or ouer-land , to the remote and fartheſt di-
ſtant quarters of the Earth, at any time within
the compaſſe of theſe 1500. yeeres: Deuided
into three ſeuerall Volumes, according to the
poſitions of the Regions, whereunto
they were directed.

This firſt Volume containing the woorthy Diſcoueries,
&c. of the Engliſh toward the North and Northeaſt by ſea,
as of *Lapland,Scrikfinia,Corelia,*the Baie of *S. Nicolas,* the Iſles of *Col-
goieue, Vaigatz,* and *Noua Zembla,* toward the great riuer *Ob,*
with the mighty Empire of *Ruſsia,*the *Caſpian* ſea,*Geor-
gia, Armenia, Media, Perſia, Boghar* in *Bactria,*
and diuers kingdoms of *Tartaria :*

Together with many notable monuments and teſtimo-
nies of the ancient forren trades, and of the warrelike and
other ſhipping of this realme of *England* in former ages.

VVhereunto is annexed alſo a briefe Commentarie of the true
ſtate of *Iſland* , and of the Northren Seas and
lands ſituate that way.

*And laſtly, the memorable defeate of the Spaniſh huge
Armada, Anno 1588.* and the famous victorie
atchieued at the citie of *Cadiz,1596.*
are deſcribed.

By RICHARD HAKLVYT *Maſter of*
Artes, and ſometime Student of Chriſt-
Church in Oxford.

Imprinted at London by GEORGE
BISHOP, RALPH NEWBERIE
and ROBERT BARKER.
1598.

The time approaches and now is that we of England may share . . . with the Spaniard and with Portugal in part of America and other regions as yet undiscovered.

In 1583, Richard went to Paris as chaplain to the English Ambassador and Walsingham briefed him to find out whatever he could about French and Spanish plans for colonies. During this intelligence work he met leading continental cosmographers and explorers. From them he learned that the English were viewed as "sluggards" in exploration. Constantly feeding back diplomatic information to Sir Francis Walsingham, Richard still found time to return home to discuss with Ralegh his Virginia scheme. The main problem was to promote interest in colonization to help finance an expedition. Aggressive propaganda was needed and so Richard wrote his *Discourse of Western Planting*, which asserted that

The Queen of England's title to all the West Indies, or at least to as much as is from Florida to the Arctic Circle, is more lawful and right than the Spaniards' or any other Christian Princes' . . . .

An English colony in the south of this region could soon outstrip Spanish colonies and provide the English with bases from which to attack Spanish treasure fleets. As Richard pointed out, Spain and Portugal had benefited enormously from their discoveries. Why should England not do the same?

To what end need I endeavour myself by arguments to prove that by this voyage our navy and navigation shall be enlarged, when as there needeth none other reason than the manifest examples of . . . the Kings of Spain and Portugal, who, since the first discovery of the Indies, have not only mightily enlarged their dominions, greatly enriched themselves and their subjects, but have also . . . trebled the number of their ships, masters and mariners . . . .

Economic advantages were obvious:

Besides this . . . a great number of men which do now live idly at home shall thereby be set at work . . . for mines and in matters of husbandry and likewise in hunting the whale; besides in fishing . . . and felling of trees . . . and suchlike work meet for those persons that are no men of Art or Science.

English trade would benefit:

. . . all Savages . . . so as they shall taste civility, will take marvellous delight in any garment . . . as a shirt, a blue, yellow, red or green cotton cassock, a cap, or such like, and will take incredible pains for such a trifle . . . .
. . . what vent for our English clothes will thereby ensue and how great benefit to Clothiers, Woolmen, Carders, Spinners, Weavers, Fullers etc. . .

44 (left) The title-page of Richard Hakluyt's *Principal Navigations*, a work which records the details of all the voyages of the Elizabethan "sea dogs". It was an inspiration to countless English sailors, explorers and navigators.

45 Thomas Cavendish was an English explorer and navigator who, between July 1586 and September 1588, became the second Englishman to circumnavigate the world.

and there would be benefits for the savages too:

First and chiefly, in respect of the most happy and gladsome tidings of the most glorious Gospel of our Saviour, Jesus Christ . . .
    . . . being brought from brutish ignorance to civility and knowledge and made to understand how the tenth part of their land may be manured and employed, as it may yield more commodities to the necessary use of man's life, than the whole now doth . . . .

Elizabeth was won over to the idea and Ralegh's Virginia scheme was launched.

After 1585, war with Spain made exploration more difficult yet this national danger only spurred Hakluyt on to assemble documents and oral accounts of all the voyages and achievements of English mariners, which he dedicated to Walsingham and published in 1589 as *The Principal Navigations, Voyages and Discoveries of the English Nation*, an immediate best-seller and one of the greatest books of the Elizabethan period. A sense of patriotism burned brightly in him as he told the stirring tales of England's maritime achievements under Elizabeth.

    . . . in searching the most opposite corners and quarters of the world, and . . . in compassing the vast globe of the earth more than once, [The English] have excelled all the nations and peoples of the earth.

Perhaps even more than men like Drake, Hawkins and Ralegh, it was Richard Hakluyt who gave the English a stronger feeling of national pride and identity. His work surpassed all previous geographical collections, recording for posterity the achievements of the early explorers.

In 1588, Richard returned to England to become Rector of Wetheringsett, devoting much of his free time to advising explorers and preparing maps for their voyages. He was later instrumental in setting up the East India Company. He died in 1616 and was buried in Westminster Abbey.

Sir Walter Ralegh (1554-1618)

Walter Ralegh is one of the best known of Elizabethan figures and yet how much do we really know about him? Much that is legendary surrounds his rise to power. Ralegh was a ruthless swashbuckler whose success at Elizabeth's court owed little to specific qualities and was more a result of his many-sidedness and native wit.

He had a good presence in a well-compacted person; a strong natural wit and a better judgment, with a bold and plausible tongue, whereby he could set out his points to best advantage.

Elizabeth was not deceived by his outrageous flattery but she found him entertaining, calling him "Warter" because of his rich Devon accent, or "the Shepherd of the Ocean" because of his reputation as a maritime adventurer. He was never lost for an elegant reply, and in turn called her "Cynthia" after the moon goddess.

Elizabeth began to be taken with his elocution and loved to hear his reasons to her demands; and the truth is, she took him for a kind of oracle, which nettled them all.

Once she asked him, "when will you cease to be a beggar?" and Walter replied, "when you cease to be a benefactress". Tradition

ÆTATIS SVÆ 34
AN 1588

AMOR ET VIRTUTE

records the incident where the young Ralegh used a diamond to scratch these words on a window pane: "Fain, would I climb, yet I fear to fall." It is said Elizabeth scratched the

46 Sir Walter Ralegh was at once explorer, poet, scientist and courtier, yet he was also an unscrupulous intriguer and one of the most unpopular men in England.

reply, "If thy heart fail thee, climb not at all".

Yet this romantic hero, this bejewelled courtier who spent a fortune on his clothes, was also an unscrupulous schemer who was hated by many of his contemporaries. His arrogance was such that he cared nothing for those who abused him.

If any man accuses me to my face, I will answer him with my mouth. But my tail is good enough to return any answer to such who traduces me behind my back.

If his ideas on colonial settlement and empire were ahead of his time, his ruthless methods and single-minded determination to reach the top on a ladder of his fallen rivals made him very much a man of his times. For all his brilliance Elizabeth never really trusted him.

Ralegh was a Devon man, from a wealthy family and was half-brother to Humphrey Gilbert. Educated at Oxford, he rejected the life of a scholar for a life of adventure, fighting for the Protestant cause in France, and helping Gilbert prepare an expedition for North America. Yet Ralegh was also studying law and turning his hand to poetry and drama, becoming involved in a brilliant circle of young men which included Philip Sidney and Richard Hakluyt.

Ralegh did further military service under Lord Grey of Wilton in Ireland, earning a reputation as a cruel but efficient soldier, massacring a garrison of Catholic troops at Smerwick. In 1581 Walter got the opportunity he had been waiting for: Grey sent him to London with despatches. Ralegh declined to return, instead offering himself to the Privy Council as an expert on Irish affairs. Grey was furious but Walter made the most of his chance, winning the attention of the Queen by his extravagant clothing and his elegant behaviour.

This Captain Ralegh coming out of Ireland to the English court in good habit (his clothes then being a considerable part of his estate) found the Queen walking, till, meeting with a plashy place, she seemed to scruple going thereon.

Presently Ralegh cast and spread his new plush cloak on the ground; whereon the Queen trod gently over, rewarding him afterwards with many suits for his so free and seasonable tender of so fair a foot cloth.

He soon became Elizabeth's new favourite, gaining estates in Ireland, a monopoly on wine licenses and the export of broadcloth, a knighthood, the office of Warden of the Stannaries (Cornish tin mines) and the title of Lord Lieutenant of Cornwall. In 1584 he became the MP for Cornwall and in 1587 he became the Captain of Elizabeth's Guard. His rise was meteoric, the fastest of any of Elizabeth's courtiers, but he had been fortunate. A German visitor commented,

She is said to love this gentleman now beyond all the others. And this must be true, because two years ago he could scarcely keep one servant, and now, with her bounty, he can keep five hundred.

During the 1580s Walter worked with Humphrey Gilbert on plans for the colonization of the New World, but he suffered from the fact that Elizabeth would not let him leave court, stopping him sailing on Gilbert's fateful voyage of 1583, in which Newfoundland was taken over but Gilbert drowned. Nevertheless, Walter gained his half-brother's patent for exploration and colonization:

. . . our trusty and well-beloved servant Walter Ralegh Esquire . . . to discover, search, find out and view such remote, heathen and barbarous lands, countries and territories, not actually possessed of any Christian prince . . . .

With the backing of Richard Hakluyt, Ralegh persuaded the Queen to support his scheme for a colony in Virginia but he was again prevented, this time from joining Sir Richard Grenville on his voyage to set up Ralph Lane as Governor of the settlement at Roanoke Island. Instead he was given the empty title of "Lord and Governor of Virginia". Although the colony failed and the settlers had to be brought home by Drake in

47 Sir Richard Grenville was a close friend of Ralegh and helped establish his first Virginia colony.

48 John White's drawing of Indians fishing off the coast of Roanoke in Virginia, drawn during Grenville and Ralegh's second expedition in 1585.

1586, a start had been made thanks to Ralegh's vision.

During the crisis of 1588, with England threatened by the Armada, Ralegh was frustrated to find himself ashore with his cousin Richard Grenville, organizing the land forces of the West Country against a possible landing. As a result he missed much of the action which won so much glory for men like Hawkins, Drake and Frobisher.

Although Ralegh's fame was enormous he was also "the best-hated man of the world, in court, city and country". After his appointment as Warden of the Cinque Ports, a letter was sent to Lord Burghley, claiming

. . . no man is more hated than him; none cursed more daily by the poor . . . . His pride is intolerable . . . .

Ralegh was credited with introducing potatoes from the New World as an aphrodisiac, as well as tobacco. Although he never actually set foot on American soil, his achievements had become legendary. Elizabeth remarked of tobacco that she had heard of men,

. . . who turned gold into smoke, but Ralegh was the first who turned smoke into gold.

But the arrival at court of young Robert Devereux, Earl of Essex, presented a challenge to Ralegh as the Queen's favourite. Quarrels between the two men were common and in 1589 Ralegh retired to his estates in Ireland, devoting himself to writing poetry and encouraging the young poet Edmund Spenser to publish *The Faerie Queene*. Walter's secret

49 Plain tobacco had been introduced into England by Sir John Hawkins in 1565, yet by the end of Elizabeth's reign tobacco smoking was associated in the public mind with Sir Walter Ralegh. Under James I the habit of smoking was condemned.

50 Ralegh married Bess Throckmorton, one of the Queen's ladies-in-waiting, secretly in 1592. They were both sent to the Tower when Elizabeth discovered.

marriage to Bess Throckmorton, one of the Queen's maids-of-honour, earned him, as so many others had found, the Queen's fury. Both he and his new wife were sent to cool off in the Tower of London. Elizabeth was slow to forgive him and never forgave his wife.

During his retirement from court life, Ralegh planned an expedition to Guiana (now Venezuela) in South America in the hope of finding the legendary land of gold: El Dorado. In 1595 he sailed with four ships, exploring the coast of Trinidad and sailing up the Orinoco, finding ore later declared worthless and returning to a poor welcome in England. It seemed the bubble of his popularity had well and truly burst. He was even accused of not having been to Guiana and in response wrote his book *The Discovery of the Large, Rich*

and Beautiful Empire of Guiana. Here he describes the alligators he encountered.

Upon this river . . . we saw divers sorts of strange fish and . . . . Lagartos . . . there were thousands of those ugly serpents . . . I had a Negro, a very proper young fellow, that leaping out of the galley to swim in the mouth of this river was in all our sights taken and devoured by one of these Lagartos . . . .

In 1596, at least partly returned to favour, Ralegh joined Essex and Howard in the attack on Cadiz. Sailing in the *Warspite*, Ralegh had the frustration of seeing the headstrong Essex burn Cadiz but lose the spoils and fail to capture the Spanish fleet. Although the raid boosted England's prestige it added little to the Queen's coffers.

Ralegh's hopes of winning back the Queen's confidence or becoming a Privy Councillor were dashed. One of his poems reveals his bitterness.

Say to the Court it glows
And shines like rotten wood;
Say to the Church it shows
What's good and doth no good.
If Church and Court reply,
Then give them both the lie.

During the Essex rebellion of 1601 Ralegh was safely entrenched with the Cecil faction and celebrated the death of his rival. But the death of Elizabeth so shortly afterwards prevented Ralegh from regaining his position as favourite. On the accession of James I, Walter lost his post as Captain of the Guard and was put on trial for high treason. The enemies he had kept at bay during Elizabeth's lifetime were now too strong for him. Found guilty of plotting against the King he was imprisoned and sentenced to death. The sentence was suspended for 13 years and during his imprisonment Ralegh wrote his great *History of the World*, as well as much poetry. In 1616 he was released to lead another expedition to Guiana to seek for gold, in the hope of regaining royal favour. But he failed and was executed on his return, a man who for so long had been ahead of his time, died as the last remnant of the Elizabethan age.

GLOSSARY

abdicate   act of giving up throne

arquebus   early musket

assassination   murder of a political or religious leader

atheist   someone who does not believe in any god

bankruptcy   inability to pay debts

circumnavigation   travel around the world

conservative   someone who does not welcome change

consort   husband or wife of ruling monarch

cosmographer   someone who maps the earth and stars

Dauphin   heir to French throne

debasement   reduction of precious metal content in coinage

excommunicate   to cut off from the sacraments of the Church

faction   division, often political or religious following for an individual leader

favourite   someone who receives favoured treatment from a ruler

heretic   someone who rejects the teaching of the Catholic Church

humanist   student of human not divine affairs

inflation   increase in the quantity of money and consequent decrease in its value

Jesuit   Catholic priest, member of Society of Jesus

masque   a play with music

missionary   someone sent to a foreign country to make religious converts

monopoly   grant by Crown of sole right to make or distribute certain products

patronage   giving financial or influential support to a person or cause

Presbyterian   follower of a Church governed by elders all of equal rank

privateer   person commissioned by their government to attack and rob foreign merchant ships

Protestant   a Christian who does not accept Catholicism

Puritan   extreme Protestant who wanted to purify the church of the last remnants of Roman Catholic ritual

radical   extremist

recusant   Catholic who refuses to attend Church of England services

regent   someone who rules during minority of a king or queen

renaissance   rebirth of learning; revival of interest in classical civilization, notably in Italy in the fifteenth and sixteenth centuries

revels   entertainment

schism   split, often within a religion

sedition   speech or writing likely to incite riots

toleration   allowing people to practise other religious beliefs

treason   offences committed against a ruler or against the state

BIOGRAPHICAL NOTES

Cardinal William Allen (1532-94). Most important English Catholic outside England. Founded colleges at Douai and Rheims to train missionary priests. Regarded as traitor and plotted with Mary Stuart.

Edward Alleyn (1566-1626). Actor and founder of Dulwich College. Member of Lord Admiral's Men, rival of Richard Burbage, played greatest roles of Marlowe and Shakespeare.

Sir Francis Bacon (1561-1626). Lawyer, courtier, author, statesman and philosopher. Spoke against his patron Essex at his trial in 1600.

Richard Bancroft (1544-1610). Bishop of London and later Archbishop of Canterbury. Supported work of Whitgift and was strong opponent of Puritanism.

William Byrd (1543-1623). Organist and composer. Although an open Catholic his loyalty was never questioned. The most important English composer of the age.

William Camden (1551-1623). Antiquary, historian and headmaster of Westminster School from 1593. Published *Annals* of Elizabeth's reign in 1615 and *Britannia*, earliest topography of the British Isles.

Thomas Cavendish (1560-92). Explorer, seaman and second English circumnavigator of world.

Robert Cecil (1563-1612). Statesman, son of Lord Burghley. Largely responsible for peaceful accession of James I.

John Davis (1550-1605). Navigator and explorer. Tried

to find north-west passage. Fought against Armada in 1588. Discovered Falkland Islands.

John Dee (1527-1608). Astrologer, mathematician, geographer and diarist. With Hakluyt he helped many English explorers including Frobisher, Drake and Ralegh. Finest mathematician of the age, combined genuine science with charlatanism.

Sir Francis Drake (1542-96). Explorer, circumnavigator and greatest sailor of the age. Scourge of Spain and symbol of English maritime power. Legend in his own time.

Sir Humphrey Gilbert (1539-83). Navigator, explorer. Half-brother to Ralegh, he was an early advocate of colonial expansion, annexed Newfoundland but drowned during expedition sent to set up colony in North America.

Robert Greene (1560-92). Dramatist, poet and pamphleteer, first to depict English low life in fiction.

Sir Richard Grenville (1541-91). Naval commander and explorer. Planted American colony at Roanoke. Died heroically in *Revenge* fighting Spaniards.

Sir Thomas Gresham (1519-79). Merchant, financier and founder of the Royal Exchange. Author of "Gresham's Law" that bad money drives out good. Advised Elizabeth on revaluation of coinage.

Sir Christopher Hatton (1540-91). Courtier and Lord Chancellor. One of Elizabeth's favourites, and a patron of arts.

Sir John Hawkins (1532-95). Naval Commander and administrator. A loyal and devoted servant of Elizabeth he was among the most important seamen of the sixteenth century. First a slaver and pirate, he was later responsible for the reconstruction of the English Navy and fought against the Armada.

Richard Hooker (1554-1600). Theologian. Defended Anglican Church settlement against Puritan and Catholic critics. Known as "Judicious Hooker", author of *The Laws of Ecclesiastical Polity*, one of the greatest works of the age.

Lord Charles Howard of Effingham (1536-1624). Admiral, commanded English fleet against the Armada in 1588.

Ben Jonson (1572-1637). Poet, dramatist and friend of Shakespeare. Virtual Poet Laureate from 1616.

William Lambarde (1536-1601). Antiquary and historian. Keeper of the Records in the Tower of London.

Robert Parsons (1546-1610). Jesuit. Accompanied Campion on his fateful mission but escaped his fate. Regarded Elizabeth as a heretic and, unlike Campion, was prepared to work for her overthrow. He was a politician in priest's garb and was the power behind the English Catholic exiles.

William Shakespeare (1564-1616). Poet, dramatist, actor. Foremost writer of the Elizabethan age and greatest figure in English literature. Friend of Richard Burbage for whom he wrote some of his most important roles.

Edmund Spenser (1552-99). Poet and friend of Sir Philip Sidney; author of *The Faerie Queene*.

Thomas, Earl of Sussex (1526-83). Statesman. A competent administrator, he suppressed the Northern Revolt in 1569. He was an opponent of Leicester on the Privy Council.

Sir Francis Walsingham (1532-90). Statesman and Secretary of State. He was one of Elizabeth's greatest ministers and worked tirelessly with Burghley to remove the Catholic threat to England. An ardent Puritan he broke the plots which threatened Elizabeth's life.

Peter Wentworth (1530-96). Puritan parliamentary leader. He defended the liberties of Parliament against the royal prerogative and was imprisoned for his stand on freedom of speech.

DATE LIST

1533	Birth of Elizabeth Tudor.
1536	Execution of Ann Boleyn.
1547	Edward VI becomes King.
1553	Mary Tudor becomes Queen.
1558	Elizabeth I becomes Queen. Loss of Calais.
1559	Acts of Supremacy and Uniformity. Treaty of Cateau-Cambresis. Treaty of Edinburgh.
1561	Mary Stuart returns from France to Scotland.
1563	Thirty-Nine Articles. Statute of Artificers.
1565	Marriage of Mary Stuart to Lord Darnley.
1566	Birth of James VI of Scotland.
1568	Mary Stuart flees to England. Seizure of Spanish treasure ships. Trade with
	Netherlands suspended.
1569	Northern Rebellion.
1570	Excommunication of Elizabeth I by Pope Pius V.
1571	Ridolfi Plot.
1572	Norfolk executed. Burghley Lord Treasurer. Massacre of St Bartholomew.
1573	Drake raids Panama. Walsingham Principal Secretary.
1574	First Seminary priests arrive in England.
1575	Grindal Archbishop of Canterbury.
1576	Frobisher's first voyage.
1577-80	Drake's circumnavigation.
1580	Jesuit mission to England. Campion executed.
1583	Whitgift Archbishop of Canterbury.

BOOK LIST

A.L. Beier, *The Problem of the Poor in Tudor and Early Stuart England*, Methuen, 1983

C. Cross, *Church and People 1450-1660*, Fontana, 1976

S. Doran, *England and Europe 1485-1603*, Longman Seminar Studies, 1986

A. Dures, *English Catholicism 1558-1642*, Longman Seminar Studies, 1983

G.R. Elton, *England under the Tudors*, Methuen, 1974

A. Fletcher, *Tudor Rebellions*, Longman Seminar Studies, 1974

A. Fraser, *Mary Queen of Scots*, Weidenfeld and Nicolson, 1969

C. Haigh, *Elizabeth I*, Longman, 1988

C. Haigh, *The Reign of Elizabeth I*, Macmillan, 1984

P. Johnson, *Elizabeth I, A Study in Power and Intellect*, Weidenfeld, 1974

N.L. Jones, *Faith by Statute*, Royal Historical Society, 1982

G. Mattingly, *The Defeat of the Spanish Armada*, Cape, 1959

J.E. Neale, *Queen Elizabeth*, Cape, 1934

D.M. Palliser, *The Age of Elizabeth 1547-1603*, Longman, 1983

C. Read, *Mr Secretary Cecil and Queen Elizabeth*, Cape, 1955

C. Read, *Lord Burghley and Queen Elizabeth*, Cape, 1960

G.B. Regan, *Elizabeth I*, Cambridge University Press, 1988

A.L. Rowse, *The England of Elizabeth*, Macmillan, 1950

A.G.R. Smith, *The Emergence of a Nation State 1529-1660*, Longman, 1984

A.G.R. Smith, *The Government of Elizabethan England*, Arnold, 1967

N. Williams, *All the Queen's Men*, Cardinal, 1974

N. Williams, *The Sea Dogs*, Weidenfeld and Nicolson, 1975

J.D. Wilson, *Life in Shakespeare's England*, Penguin, 1968

INDEX